The Complete Beginner's Guide to Bicycling

The Complete Beginner's
Guide to
BICYCLING

RICHARD B. LYTTLE

Doubleday & Company, Inc., Garden City, New York   1974

ISBN: 0-385-04939-0 Trade
0-385-06259-1 Prebound
Library of Congress Catalog Card Number 73–80947
Copyright © 1974 by Richard B. Lyttle
All Rights Reserved
Printed in the United States of America
First Edition

This book is for
KEENE and HELEN HALDEMAN

Acknowledgments

Individuals assisting in the collection of information and pictures for this book were Officer Keith E. Chapman of the California Highway Patrol, James L. Konski of the Onondaga Cycling Club, T. Robert Mayer of the Baltimore Cycling Club, W. R. Pearson of the North Roads Bicycle Club, and Lawrence Reade of the Buffalo Cycling Club. Organizations contributing information and pictures were American Youth Hostels, Inc., Boy Scouts of America, the Bicycle Institute of America, the California State Automobile Association, the International Bicycle Touring Society, the National Safety Council, Schwinn Bicycle Company, and the United States Bicycle Polo Association. I gratefully acknowledge this help. In addition, many thanks are due Edward F. Dolan, Jr., and Barthold Fles for advice and support. Finally, for Jean, who has pedaled many miles without complaint, my deepest thanks.

Contents

PART I
All About Bicycles

1. Fun on Wheels

Over the past decade, Americans have seen the popularity of the bicycle soar at an astounding rate. The boom has swept the country from coast to coast. Since 1960, more than 75 million new bikes have been put into service. In 1974, Americans are expected to spend $516 million on bicycles. And the boom continues, with both foreign and domestic manufacturers struggling to meet the ever-growing demand.

The boom is truly astounding, but today, with every other American owning a bike or at least appreciating its virtues, astonishment is giving way to puzzlement. Why weren't bikes always popular?

Engineers regard the bicycle as the most efficient mode of transportation devised by man. Indeed in Europe, particularly Denmark and Holland, the bike has long served as a leading means of private transportation. There are sound reasons for this.

Bikes are relatively cheap, and with proper care they can last a lifetime. They do not take acres of parking space. They do not belch toxic fumes. They make no noise above a whisper. They do not run up appalling maintenance bills, and you do not have to feed them hay, coal, gasoline, or Diesel oil.

Doctors concerned with the rising toll of heart disease look upon the bicycle as a lifesaver for deskbound executives and a tool for better health in general. Pedaling a bicycle, the doctors say, is on a par with jogging or swimming as an all-round body conditioner. Cycling improves circulation, breathing, and digestion. It has been prescribed as a cure for back ailments, hardened arteries, lung disease, ulcers, and even psychological problems. Doctors who work with the aging say cycling can contribute to a longer, more enjoyable life. Doctors who work with children say cycling aids growth and helps build strong, healthy bodies.

Indeed, Dr. Paul Dudley White, who received national attention as President Eisenhower's heart specialist in the 1950s, probably contributed more to the bicycle boom than any other individual, when he urged Americans to cycle their way to better health. And Dr. White recognized the many other virtues of cycling and used his eloquence to praise them.

The bike opens new vistas in travel and experience. Within the glass-and-steel shell of an automobile you can speed through a country and never know its nature. On a bike you hear, smell, and observe your surroundings at leisure, and best of all, the bike provides an ideal way to meet people. A man, intimidated by the noise and smell of a car, is usually curious about a cyclist and eager to make conversation. More and more tourists are discovering that the best way to see a foreign country is by bicycle. Organized cycling tours are now available in Europe, Japan, Canada, parts of Latin America, and nearly ever state in the Union.

For many, particularly younger riders, the bike offers a chance to earn money, either simply as transportation to a job or as a vehicle for deliveries. The bike-riding newspaper boy or girl has long been a familiar part of the suburban American scene.

Cycling is good sport. Competitive racing gains each season both in entrants and spectators, and the opportunities for less demanding excitement seem limited only by the cyclist's imagination. Bicycle polo, already popular in England, is now established on America's eastern seaboard. Annual bicycle rodeos draw crowds in nearly every town and city in the country, and the variety of contests in these events assures a fair test for all, from beginner to advanced.

You can go camping with your bike, or if you prefer a roof at night, you can take advantage of youth hostels. In America and Canada, the bicycle boom has brought the youth-hostel movement from a slow start to full bloom.

You can join a bicycle club, and your club can sponsor races and tours, promote construction of new bicycle paths, and work toward improved safety standards and facilities. If there is no club in your community, which today seems un-likely, you can start your own club. All the existing clubs, by the way, are eager for junior members.

The list of cycling virtues goes on and on, but one virtue not yet mentioned is probably the most important of all: Cycling is fun.

How do you describe your satisfaction at speeding under your own power four times as fast as a man can walk? You certainly cannot measure such satisfaction. And you do not measure the pride you feel at topping a difficult hill or com-pleting a distance that once seemed awesome. Self-reliance and responsibility ride with you on your bike. The bike gives independence and status. All these things, elusive and hard to measure as they are, can put fun in your life.

Little wonder that the cycling public of today asks why the bicycle was not always popular!

Of course, timely urgings such as those of Dr. White were significant in calling attention to the bicycle, and its clean qualities have aided its acceptance in an era of growing con-cern over air and noise pollution, but the real reason for the bicycle boom can be found in the machine itself. And when we see how slow the evolution of the modern bicycle has been, particularly in America, we can understand why it has just begun to take the place it deserves.

A generation ago, the bicycle was a heavy, single-geared device with road-dragging balloon tires, and it usually came from the factory overloaded with unnecessary accessories. While these sturdy bikes still have a use, the prospective bi-cycle buyer of today has a marvelous range of selection, every-thing from a novelty high-rise bike to a three-speed utility bike, from an adult tricycle to a light *dérailleur* with a fifteen-speed gear selection.

It was not until the early 1960s that chain stores in this

country began offering European-style, lightweight bikes. It was not until the early 1960s that domestic manufacturers began offering novelty bikes to an eager market. These two moves alone brought far more success than any chain-store executive or factory owner had imagined. The time was certainly ripe. The time, in fact, was late.

While this retarded marketing and manufacturing condition goes far to explain the late blooming of bike popularity in America, there are other things that have limited and will continue to limit full acceptance of the bike. These are its faults, and even though the virtues far outweigh the faults, you should know what is wrong with a bike.

THE BAD MARKS

The most serious charge is that the bicycle is unsafe. It is true that bicycles and automobiles do not mix well. Autos can go much faster, and in a collision the cyclist invariably suffers the most harm. These are good reasons for cautious cycling, but, unfortunately, well over half of the cycling accidents recorded in growing numbers each year are the fault of the cyclist. Is the machine really unsafe? Isn't it, instead, the person who operates it?

Another charge against the bike is that it is prized by thieves. Little can be done to stop a determined thief, and the stolen bike is all too easy for the thief to sell. Most household insurance policies cover such thefts; if not, you can buy coverage for under ten dollars a year for a hundred-dollar bike. While you can recover your loss, insurance does nothing to stop thieves. Though far from perfect, the best theft retardant is a stout chain and solid lock.

Of course, the bike has other, obvious limits. You will probably not want to ride it in a snowstorm, and you might not enjoy it if you try loading it with too much luggage. But enthusiastic cyclists look on such limitations as challenges. Those who have pedaled through bad storms often remember the struggle as a high point in their cycling experience. Those who camp or tour often boast about how much they can do without and how light and compact they can make the luggage they do carry.

What else is wrong with the bike? I have listed all I know. Perhaps you can think of more, but chances are, as your cycling experience grows, you will have a hard time counting faults, while your list of bicycling virtues will seem endless.

Here, for instance, is a virtue yet unmentioned. Learning to ride is easy. Before discussing learning methods, though, it would be best to study the anatomy of a bicycle.

BIKE PARTS

The frame of a boys' bicycle is made of hollow metal tubing, with the three strongest members forming a triangle. The horizontal top tube meets the seat tube at the back side of the triangle, which joins the down tube at the front side of the triangle. A horizontal cylinder perpendicular to the frame marks the junction of the seat tube and the down tube. It is called the bottom bracket. A short, almost vertical tube links the top tube and the down tube. It is called the steering head. A tube called the stem fits inside the steering head and turns on ball-bearing collars top and bottom. The stem rises to a gooseneck that holds the handlebars. Immediately below the steering head, the stem is attached to the fork at a junction called the fork crown. The two arms of the fork are slotted at their tips to hold the front wheel axle. The rear wheel axle is supported by two pairs of arms. One pair, extending almost horizontally from the bottom bracket, is made up of the chain stays. The other pair, slanting down from the junction of the top tube and the seat tube, is made up of the seat stays. These stays meet in slotted plates on either side of the wheel, a junction referred to as the rear drop-out.

The bike wheel has a tire, rim, spokes (usually thirty-six), hub, and axle. In addition, the rear-wheel hub has a toothed sprocket on the right side. Sides of a bike are given as you face forward, looking from back to front of the bike.

The power drive of a bike begins with pedals and cranks on either side of the bottom bracket. These are joined by the

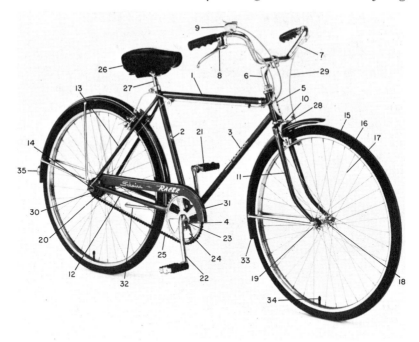

The parts of a bike are as follows: 1. top tube, 2. seat tube, 3. down tube, 4. bottom bracket, 5. steering head, 6. stem, 7. handlebars, 8. brake lever, 9. gear trigger, 10. crown, 11. fork, 12. chain stay, 13. seat stay, 14. rear drop-out, 15. tire, 16. rim, 17. spokes, 18. hub, 19. axle, 20. wheel sprocket, 21. pedal, 22. crank, 23. crank axle, 24. chain wheel or sprocket, 25. chain, 26. seat, 27. seat post, 28. caliper brake, 29. brake cable, 30. three-speed hub, 31. chain guard, 32. kick stand, 33. fender, 34. valve stem, 35. reflector. Courtesy Schwinn Bicycle Company

crank axle, which rides inside the bracket on a set of cups and bearings. The large, toothed wheel on the right-hand side of the bottom bracket is called the chain wheel or chain sprocket, and the chain itself leads from this to the rear-wheel sprocket.

The bicycle seat, or saddle, is clamped to the top of the seat post, which fits inside the seat tube. Seat angle and height as well as handlebar angle and height can be adjusted to fit individual owners.

The most popular braking system on today's bike is made

up of calipers fitted to the frame above each wheel. Handlebar levers and cables control the calipers. Pressure on the
grips brings small shoes on the arms of the calipers against
the rim of the wheel.

Later on, when we see the variations in bike style and design, we will see that few bikes look exactly like the one pictured here. A girls' bike will usually have two drop tubes, instead of a top tube. This bike has caliper brakes, but some have
coaster brakes, contained in the rear hub. This bike has a
three-speed rear hub with trigger control on the handlebars.
There are many other gear systems, including dérailleurs,
with multiple wheel sprockets and chain sprockets. But despite the variety, the basic nomenclature for all bikes remains
the same.

LEARNING TO RIDE

You may already know how to ride. If at an early age you
were lucky enough to have a beginners' bike with training
wheels, you learned to ride in the best way possible. Starting
later in life, after you have outgrown the beginners' model,
takes a little more courage and determination. Of course, you
will not become a skilled cyclist simply by reading this book,
but the learning method described here has helped many beginners through those first difficulties. Actually, most beginners
are soon happily surprised to discover how easy it all is.

First, a word about fit. Too many beginners try to learn on
bikes that are too big for them. If you straddle the top tube
and cannot get your feet firmly on the ground, the bike is too
big, even dangerous. You need a smaller bike, and I suggest
you lower the seat far enough so that you can plant both feet
flat on the ground. You will want to raise the seat later for more
efficient pedaling, but in the beginning, the low seat will help
build confidence. Buying before learning, I feel, is a mistake
made all too often. How can you know what bike is right for
you until after you have learned to ride?

It is far better to borrow a friend's bike, and if you are
lucky, the friend will help you.

The beginner's biggest worry when he first mounts a bike is balance. The worry makes him hesitant, and this leads to trouble. A bike becomes stable only when it is moving.

Consider a coin. You can balance it on edge, but it takes a steady hand, and the slightest nudge will topple it. But when you roll the coin, even if you do it casually, it will stay on edge, bounce over bumps, jump from table to floor and continue upright until it has lost momentum. It begins to wobble only as it slows.

Beginning bike riders often start too slowly, and the bike, just like the coin, is unstable.

If you have a friend to help steady the bike, you can, of course, begin slowly without fear of falling. If you are alone, start practicing on a slight slope. That will give you the forward motion needed for stability.

Later, when you gain a little confidence, you should practice at low speed. If the bike leans to the right, turn the handlebars slightly to the right. If the bike leans left, turn slightly left. This corrects the lean at once, and when you learn to do this instinctively, you have mastered the art of balance. However, do not expect to attain this skill in your first practice session. The first session should be devoted to coasting down the slope. Take one thing at a time.

At first you should concentrate on steering in a straight line. Let your feet drag if you wish, but soon, for the sake of your shoes and improving your skill, you must place your feet on the pedals. When you can keep the bike coasting in a straight line, try turning the pedals. Take this slowly if it make you nervous, but try not to look down at your feet. Your eyes should be straight ahead. That is the safe way to cycle. In addition, looking down tends to disturb the sense of balance for some beginners.

Eventually you will be able to pedal with increased force, able to extend your distance well beyond the point where the practice slope levels off. You have learned to move the bike under your own power. You are ready to practice braking.

With both coaster and caliper brakes, you must develop a gentle touch. With hard back pressure on coaster brakes, the rear wheel will grab, the tire will skid, and you might take a spill. The levers for caliper brakes should be squeezed gradually. You must feel them out to learn just how much pressure is required to bring the bike to a stop at various speeds. Use both front and rear caliper brakes in unison. Shoes wear evenly that way, and of course, the brakes are twice as efficient than when applied singly. At high speed, incidentally, you can flip a bike by applying the front brake alone, but let's hope you don't hit such speeds as a novice.

While still using the practice slope, you should learn to make turns. For many beginners, this is the most difficult step. Again, the temptation is to slow the bike too much. You will want to slow some for sharp turns, but you should begin with very shallow turns. These can be managed without braking. Lean your weight slightly in the direction of the turn, and at the same time make just a small shift in the handlebars. Recover from the turn with a lean, and shift in the other direction. In your first few attempts, you might want to drag a foot while turning, but this will make it difficult to gain the knack of leaning or banking with your turns. As your ability improves, try sharper and sharper turns. At the bottom of the slope, try turning while pedaling. Take the bike in a wide turn and start back up the slope. Don't be discouraged if you don't get far on the first try. Concentrating on pedaling, turning, and balance all at once is a challenge. The trick is to keep at this until all the actions become part of the subconscious. When you have reached this stage, when it begins to feel as if you and the bike move as a single unit, then you are ready to leave the practice slope and work on level ground.

Starting on the level appears more difficult than it is. You simply have to get the bike moving at enough speed for stability. Before getting on the bike, position one pedal up, slightly forward of vertical. Now hold the handlebars firmly. Straddle the bike, and with one foot on the ground, place the other foot on the raised pedal. You are ready to start. Shove off with the ground foot and press with the pedal foot. As the bike moves forward, lift the free foot to its position on the pedal. Again, avoid looking down when you do this. Right-handers usually prefer to start with the right pedal raised; left-handers, the left pedal. Do what is the more comfortable for you. When you have mastered level starts, it is time to think about refining your cycling for improved efficiency.

If you lowered the seat for your first efforts, it is time to re-adjust it now. With a properly adjusted seat, your leg should be almost fully extended when the pedal is in the down position. Consider other adjustments as well. You should not be tense. Veteran cyclists recommend an equal distribution of weight over pedals, seat, and handlebars. The gooseneck at the top of the steering stem should be the same distance from the ground as the seat. These are guides. Do not be afraid to do a little experimenting to find what is best for you. You may discover that no amount of adjustment makes the bike feel right. This means the bike is not the right size or style for you. Let's hope it is a borrowed bike and not one you have just purchased.

The balls of your feet, not your heels or your insteps, should press against the pedals. This not only prevents aching feet, but it also allows you to practice the technique of ankling. This is simply flexing your foot downward as you push the pedal down and bending the foot up as the pedal rises. With the foot rocking from the ankle in this manner with each turn of the pedals, you get a bonus of power in your cycling. Foot clips give you even more power by enabling the lifting foot to pull the pedal, but you should not consider foot clips until you have fully mastered the bike. With your feet anchored to the pedals, you cannot use a leg to brace against a fall.

At this point, I should warn against overconfidence. You are still a beginner. Work up to long trips gradually. Take time to develop those cycling muscles. Otherwise, you may be in for cramps or exhaustion. And use sense going down hills. Brake frequently. Maintain a steady coasting speed. Never let yourself go too fast for full control of your bike.

With these words of warning, let's end the lesson. Now you are ready to have fun on wheels.

2. Bicycle Evolution

Knowledge of how the modern bike came to be, makes it even more appreciated. The bike has had a bumpy history.

In many ways, the history of the bicycle reads like the story of evolution. Species rose, dominated, and died off. Specialization appeared gradually. Some designs failed. Others led to new breeds, and in the end the best survived.

Of course, evolution of animals began millions of years ago. The first bike appeared less than three hundred years back.

No one can give an exact date to the first bike. A stained-glass church window at Stoke Poges, England, confuses things a bit. The window, installed in 1642, shows what appears to be a bicycle-like creation, but scholars who have examined the window at length cannot be sure if the vehicle had one wheel or two. And whatever it was might not have existed. It might have been nothing more than a product of the artist's imagination.

The first bicycle-like creation did not appear for at least another fifty years. Originating in France, it was a two-wheeled machine that the rider straddled and propelled by pushing his feet against the ground. Primitive though it was, this design survived with very few refinements for nearly a century, under names such as "walk-along," "céléripède," "bivector," "curricle," "bicipède," "accelerator," and "swift-walker."

Though sometimes as hard to pronounce as it was to ride, the machine remained unchanged until 1816, when Baron Karl Drais von Sauerbronn, of Karlsruhe, Germany, chief forester of the duchy of Baden, discovered steering. The baron, whose job took him on tours of inspection through the countryside, built a walk-along with wooden wheels and frame. The front wheel pivoted and thus saved the baron the trouble of picking up the machine and reaiming it each time he wanted to change directions.

Steering gave bike development a big boost. The new machines, known as "draisines," "hobbyhorses," and "dandy horses," started a fad and brought about Europe's first bicycle boom. Actually it was not much of a boom. You had to be young and healthy to push a dandy horse, and you had to be wealthy to buy one. The dandy-horse clubs that formed at this time were exclusive groups. And the early races hardly drew the public attention Europeans give cycling competition today. But the new interest was enough to speed up experimentation and development.

In 1819, Dennis Johnson, a London hobbyhorse maker, of-

A nineteenth-century hobbyhorse bicycle.

fered the first drop-bar frame for ladies. In 1821, the English-man Lewis Gompertz experimented with self-propulsion. One worked the Gompertz rack-and-pinion with a push of the feet, a pull on the handlebars, and a good deal of grim-jawed determination.

Though a blind alley in the evolution path, Gompertz's machine may have inspired Kirkpatrick Macmillan, a Scottish blacksmith. He produced what purists regard as the first true bicycle. It had handlebars, and pedals connected to rods that drove the front wheel. The Macmillan bike appeared about 1840 and fired new interest, particularly among young men and women. Remember, until the bike came along, private transportation was limited to the horse and buggy and shoe leather. Any trip more than a few miles from home was a big event and a big job. The bike brought the promise of extended horizons.

Bike enthusiasts, however, had many difficulties. With rough roads and no rubber tires, a ride in the country could be a teeth-chattering experience. The drivers of buggies, carriages, drays, and farm wagons generally hated the cyclists, whose machines set horses snorting, shying, or running for the barn. Angry drivers were known to steer deliberately into cycling groups.

Fortunately for our history, however, youth prevailed. Cycling interest grew, and inventive men continued to make contributions. In 1855, Ernest Michaux produced a bike with pedals and cranks attached directly to the axle of the front wheel. Ten years later, Michaux's associate, Pierre Lallement, perfected the design. Some perfection! This machine could move faster than earlier models, but a fast ride on wooden rims and iron tires over a rough road could be breath-taking, to say the least. These bikes soon became known as "bone-shakers," a name that stuck even after solid rubber tires appeared, in 1868.

Makers offered boneshakers with frames of hollow tubing and wheels with wire spokes, both distinct improvements. With each new model, the front wheel grew bigger and the rear wheel smaller. Was this an improvement? The makers and the buyers seemed to think so. The bigger driving wheel meant more speed. It also meant hard work, and as wheel size grew, the cyclist had to climb higher and higher to straddle it. Where falls once caused bruised knees and elbows, they now caused broken bones and cracked heads.

The high-wheelers, also known as "penny-farthings" or "ordinaries," originated in England about 1870. Their faults were evidently overlooked by an enthusiastic public. Perhaps the risk added romance to cycling. The fact is that demand for the high-wheelers soared, and the boom continued through the decade in America and Europe. Usually, front wheels had a diameter of fifty inches, rear wheels seventeen, but there were some makers who went to extremes, offering a model with a sixty-four-inch front wheel.

Today we can look upon high-wheelers as the dinosaurs of bicycle evolution. We marvel that men could tame such beasts. To mount a high-wheeler, the cyclist ran, pushing it ahead of him. Then, using a small step on the left side of the frame, above the rear wheel, he vaulted to the saddle and extended his feet to catch the spinning pedals. Dismounting without bruises and embarrassment called for even more skill.

A penny-farthing.

It was safest to swing to the ground before the towering machine came to a full stop. A good man could do this with grace —catch his machine with one hand and use the other to tip his hat to the ladies.

In 1877, Colonel Albert Pope, of Boston, Massachusetts, began building high-wheelers and became America's first manufacturer of bicycles. He asked and received $313 for each machine. In those days $313 was a small fortune. A man had to be an acrobat and he had to be rich to have a high-wheeler.

With high-wheelers men performed remarkable feats. The achievement of Thomas Stevens borders on the unbelievable. In 1884, Stevens rode, pushed, dragged, and carried his bicycle across the United States, from Oakland, California, to Boston, Massachusetts, in 103½ days. There were very few road maps to guide him, mainly because there were very few roads. He followed railroad beds when he could, but this nearly brought disaster. Once, when he was halfway across a river trestle, Stevens was confronted by a fast-approaching train. There was no time for argument. Stevens hung from the trestle with one arm and held his seventy-five-pound bike out of danger with the other until the train had passed. Meeting a train in a dark Sierra snow tunnel also offered excitement, but Stevens, who leaned his bike against the wall and threw himself to the ground each time he heard a train, said he soon got used to these meetings.

Coyotes chased him. Drunken cowboys in one western town taunted him. Cross winds knocked him flat. And once, when he was speeding down the eastern slope of the Rockies, the metal spoons of his brakes turned red with heat.

At Chicago and beyond, he began to meet small crowds who encouraged him on, but roads remained generally bad. He lost several hours wading through a swamp. When Stevens finally reached his goal, Boston citizens and public officials staged a reception in his much-deserved honor.

By the time of Stevens' achievement, people had become well acquainted with the faults of the high-wheeler, and manufacturers had begun a search for improved designs. In the days of long skirts, the high-wheeler did nothing to encourage lady cyclists. Tricycles for a time seemed the answer for ladies as well as short men. In the search for new breeds, one man designed a huge-wheeled machine with two small wheels as outriggers. The operator sat inside the big wheel like a bird in a cage, working a set of pedals. This, needless to say, became another evolutionary dead end. Something else had to be found.

THE NEW DESIGN

In 1885, John K. Starley, of Coventry, England, built a bike that had a front wheel just slightly larger than the rear wheel. The rider sat near the back of the frame and turned a set of pedals mounted at the bottom of the frame. A chain drive turned the rear wheel. Starley named it "rover." It was the first prototype of the modern bike.

One of Starley's early machines: the "Coventry Rotary Tricycle."

With a rover, most spills could be avoided by simply touching a foot to the ground. And with the drive linked to the rear wheel, rather than the direct front-axle arrangement of the ordinaries, steering became simpler and more accurate. Manufacturers everywhere began copying Starley's design and advertising it as the "safety bicycle." It had broader appeal, a much broader market than the high-wheeler. Cycling rapidly gained popularity. Competing manufacturers searched for improvements to get an edge in the market.

By far the greatest improvement of the day sprung from the tinkering of an Irish veterinarian. John B. Dunlop, of Belfast, liked to make things in his home workshop. He had already learned to make gloves for his surgical work by backing rubber with canvas, and when his son, Johnny, complained that the hard rubber tires on his new tricycle caused an uncomfortable ride, Dr. Dunlop decided to make inflatable "gloves" for the wheels. Dr. Dunlop used strips of linen from his wife's oldest dress as backing for the rubber. When he completed the tires, fitted them on Johnny's tricycle, and saw that they worked, Dr. Dunlop looked for other projects to keep him occupied. He evidently was not impressed with the first appearance of the pneumatic tire, but a friend was. William Hume took one look at Johnny's tricycle and urged the doctor to make a set of tires for a safety bike. Hume was president of the Belfast Cycling Club, and the club members were competitive racers. On May 18, 1889, the first bike with Dunlop tires, Hume aboard, was unveiled to the public. Hume's racing friends had a hard time inspecting it. They could not catch up, but within months of that race, every cyclist in the British Isles wanted Dunlops. The demand spread to Europe and then America. By 1891, the new tires had become standard equipment on all bikes sold. This launched the golden age of cycling.

Manufacturers could hardly keep abreast of demand. Every major city had at least one bicycle factory. In America there were four hundred bicycle makers by 1896, and, the following year, production peaked at two million machines. Makers included such men as Henry Ford, Wilbur and Orville Wright, and Glenn Curtiss.

The bicycle sparked the spirit of the "Gay Nineties." The

change in fashion alone gives a good idea of the bicycle's influence. Before women took to cycling, they wore as many as six starched petticoats and an assortment of other yardage beneath a full-length dress. Those daring enough to go swimming wore a suit of twelve yards of material.

In America the women followed French design, and the young French women were the first to wear sensible cycling clothes—a tailored skirt and shirtwaist without frills, a tight-fitting outfit that followed the contours of the female form. Victorian matrons in America were appalled, but if the French were wearing such clothes, they had to be accepted, or at least tolerated. Then knickerbockers, something like the scandalous bloomer, appeared. High stockings and boots hid the forbidden ankles, but this outfit was almost too much. Indignant men wrote letters of outrage to newspapers and politicians. It did no good. The women wanted to go cycling, and they wanted to do it in comfort. It was typical of the independence, self-assertion, and revolt that marked the era.

The cycling rage brought financial crisis. Horse breeders and stablekeepers were among the first to suffer losses. Then entertainers, jewelers and watchmakers, piano manufacturers and book publishers discovered that most of the luxury money normally spent on their goods was being invested in bicycles. It was a period of adjustment. While some businesses lost, new ones came into being, such as making tubing for bicycle frames, rims, spoke wire, and tires. Those willing to change with the times fared well.

BICYCLE CLUBS

Despite the increasing number of bicycles on the road, cyclists remained a minority. They had to be young, daring, and wealthy. The old, the conservative, and the poor resented this early-day jet set. This led to trouble.

Urchins thought it good sport to shove sticks in the spokes of a passing bike. In the country, farmers and draymen refused to move aside to let cyclists pass. If dogs needed encouragement to attack, their owners sicked them on the cyclists.

Almost from the moment bicycles appeared, politicians began legislating against them. In many cities, bicycles were banned from important streets and parks. In England the Highway and Railway Act of 1878 gave rural officials the right to invoke any rules they wished against cyclists. One rule called for the cyclist to pull off the road and stop, the moment a horse-drawn vehicle appeared. American regulations followed similar patterns. Cyclists could not use New Jersey's Haddonfield Turnpike. A man would be arrested for riding a bicycle in New York's Central Park.

The public resentment and legal restrictions brought cyclists together. They found it was safest to travel the roads in groups, and, by banding together, they gained political strength.

The British Touring Club, now called the Cyclists' Touring Club, was formed in 1878, and is recognized today as the oldest nationwide bicycle club in the world. Its *Gazette* defended the cyclists' rights, and its members fought for and finally won repeal of the Highway and Railway Act. On this side of the Atlantic, the League of American Wheelmen came into being, at Newport, Rhode Island, in 1880. Four years later, the League managed to lift the ban on the Haddonfield Turnpike, and after an eight-year court battle, opened Central Park to cyclists.

The League, along with many smaller clubs in cities and towns across the country, performed other valuable services. The best road maps of the day and the strongest demand for road improvements came from bicycle clubs. League members traveled with the best information on restaurants and lodging, and if accommodations could not be found, they knew of other league members in the region who would gladly put them up for a night. League membership peaked at 102,636 before the end of the century, but with the advent of the automobile, membership dwindled and the club finally died. The current cycling boom, however, brought it back to life, and the League of American Wheelmen stands today as the parent club in our country's cycling fraternity.

EARLY RACING

Competition offered another incentive to organize. Bicycle racing began almost from the moment two men with dandy horses met. These informal contests certainly helped prompt improvements in the bicycle.

Few reports of early races survive. America's first officially sanctioned race was won by Will R. Pitman, who pedaled his high-wheeler over a mile course in three minutes and fifty-seven seconds, just a shade slower than today's fastest time for the mile run. Speeds increased with the safety bicycle. In 1895, E. F. Leonert pedaled against a race horse over a mile course, beat the horse, and set a new record, of one minute and thirty-five seconds.

Two forms of bicycle racing rose in the nineties. In one, the cyclists vied for the best time over a measured distance. In the other, they tried to get the best distance in a set time—an hour, two hours, twelve hours, a day. The six-day bicycle race was an extension of this second form.

The first six-day race was held at the old Madison Square Garden, in 1891. William "Plugger" Martin, using a high-wheeler, won that contest, covering 1,466 miles and four laps in six days of almost constant pedaling. Six-day races drew huge crowds, and they might have continued indefinitely had it not been for one Charles Miller. Miller, using a safety bike in an 1898 race, covered a remarkable 2,093.4 miles in six days, but his blistering pace sent many of his competitors to the hospital, suffering from physical exhaustion. Public outcry followed, and after one more single-man race, in 1899, promoters discontinued the contests in favor of six-day team racing. Though the six-day team races never gained popularity in America, they did catch on in Europe and are still staged there and called "Madisons," honoring their place of origin.

Racing over a measured distance, particularly the mile, probably brought the most interest and debate during the nineties. As records continued to fall, some cyclists began to wonder what the speed limit, if any, might be. On an evening in 1899, one Charlie Murphy, an off-duty member of the Brooklyn Police Department's crack Bicycle Patrol, boasted to a tavern crowd that he could ride his bike as fast as any train in the land. The only condition he made was that he ride right behind the train, to take advantage of the draft. Murphy correctly figured that wind resistance put a big restriction on cycling speed.

For a time, no one took Murphy's boast seriously, but one day it came to the ears of Hal Fullerton, agent for the Long Island Rail Road, a man who recognized a chance for publicity. He invited the cycling policeman to make his boast good and set to work at once preparing a track. Workmen laid down planking between three miles of rail. On the back end of a caboose, carpenters constructed a windscreen. On June 30, 1899, track, train, and Murphy were ready.

Train and cyclist started a mile back from the starting line. The engine accelerated. So did Murphy, keeping within the vacuum created by the windscreen. By the time he hit the measured mile, Murphy was hitting sixty miles an hour, and at the finish line, astounded timekeepers found that he had pedaled the distance in 57.8 seconds. Ten years passed before a racing car could beat Murphy's record.

Actually, in light of subsequent events, "Mile-a-Minute" Murphy, as he became known, might have gone much faster, had the train gone faster. In 1962, France's Jose Meiffret was clocked at 127.16 miles an hour while following the draft of a car on Germany's Autobahn. That record still stands today.

THE DÉRAILLEUR

To trace further advances in bicycle design we must leave America, where the automobile all but killed the cycling fad. Middle-class youths aspired to be car owners. The bicycle simply filled that difficult age when one was too old to sit at home and too young to drive. Invariably it was a heavy machine, with balloon tires and a single-geared, coaster-brake rear hub. It survived hard use, but its popularity was limited.

In Europe, however, only the very wealthy could afford automobiles. Bicycles remained popular, and the search for improvements continued. Thus, while evolution fell into static years in the New World, it continued at a healthy pace in the Old.

English bicycle makers began experimenting with gears. One of the earliest successful arrangements was the protean gear, a split chain wheel that expanded upon partial reverse of the pedals. Later, English inventors conceived the epicycle gearing housed within the rear hub and activated by a lateral shift of the axle to engage various cogged-wheel combinations.

While the English advances were significant, the most remarkable development occurred in France. It was achieved by a remarkable man. His real name was Paul de Vivie. He started adult life as a silk merchant, but at twenty-eight he purchased a high-wheeled bicycle and became a confirmed cyclist. He mastered his awkward machine, did stunts with it, and sped around the countryside of his Saint-Étienne home at remarkable speeds.

M. de Vivie searched for better bicycles. None were made in France, so he had to cross the Channel to visit shops in England. The next step was inevitable. In 1887 he sold his silk business, opened a shop, and began importing English bikes. To promote cycling, he began publishing a magazine. In *Le Cycliste*, as it was called, M. de Vivie signed all his articles with "Velocio," and that was how he soon became known both to his friends and the public.

Velocio made his first bicycle in 1889. It failed to satisfy him, mainly because the single gear restricted hill climbing. He built a bike with two concentric chain wheels. To change to a lower gear, he had to stop and lift the chain from the larger to the smaller wheel. It was primitive, but this was the first dérailleur bicycle. In 1901, Velocio produced a bike combining the English, protean design with his own. Unfortunately, Velocio's shop, his writing, and his inventing kept him so busy he neglected to take out patents. By 1908, four other French firms were producing dérailleur bicycles and claiming the invention as their own.

Velocio used his considerable writing talents to advocate gears. His Chemineau bike, brought out in 1906, was remarkably like the modern dérailleur, but, strangely, cyclists resisted gears. The purists attacked the gear concept, claiming use of gears showed weakness. Velocio was near the end of his career before gearing became generally accepted in Europe.

On February 27, 1930, at age seventy-seven, Velocio was pushing his bike through heavy traffic not far from his home when a car struck and killed him. To this day, Frenchmen gather yearly at Saint-Étienne for a bicycle rally in honor of Velocio, the remarkable man who introduced modern cycling to the world.

3. Your Bike

A glance through a bicycle catalogue or a brief visit to a bicycle shop will be enough to tell you of the great changes that have come to pass since the wooden-wheeled dandy horses bounced the cobblestone streets of Europe.

Dérailleur systems, though they attract much discussion and inspection, are not the only thing to consider in selecting a bike. In fact, a dérailleur might not suit your needs at all. How you select a bike, what you look for in quality, what style is right for you, and some hard facts about bike prices will be the subject of this chapter. Basically, selection comes down to your size, your physical ability, and the uses you plan for your machine.

You can buy the finest, most expensive bike made and be terribly disappointed if you fail to pay careful attention to size. This is silly. Standard frame and wheel sizes cover such a range that you are certain, with a little patience, to find the right bike for you.

Your most important measurement is not your height, but the length of your leg. That is the inside measurement of your leg from crotch to ground. The most important measurement on the bike is the distance between the top bar and the ground. You should be able to straddle the top bar with both feet on the ground and have at least half an inch clearance between your crotch and the top bar. The clearance provides an important safeguard against injury. On a girls' bike, though the possibility of injury is not a factor, use the same standard of measurement on an imaginary line between steering head and seat tube, where a top bar would be if the bike were a boys' model.

Frame and wheel size determine the height of the top bar. Wheel diameters range from twelve inches on the tiny-tot bikes to twenty-eight inches on adult models. Most dérailleurs have twenty-seven-inch wheels. Frame sizes, measured on the length of the seat tube, range from eight inches on tiny-tot models to twenty-four inches and sometimes more on adult bikes.

If you have legs of normal muscular development and strength, it is best to reduce the frame size before taking a reduction in wheel size to get the combination that will give the proper clearance above the top tube.

What about seat height? Here again, your inside leg measurement is the key. You can add 10 per cent to this measurement and theoretically come up with the proper distance between the top of the saddle and the down-positioned pedal. This should give you the most efficient leg extension in pedaling. If your knees remain bent while pedaling, you not only fail to take advantage of full power potential, but you also run the risk of fatigue and cramps. Actually more important than theory is feel. The height of the seat should feel right to you. Seat height can be adjusted easily by loosening the clamp nut at the top of the seat tube and sliding the seat post up or down. Reset the clamp nut firmly after the adjustment. Most saddles can be adjusted fore and aft and by angle through loosening the clamp nut holding the seat to the post. The nose of the saddle should be from one and a half to two inches back from an imaginary vertical line bisecting the bottom bracket. Normally the angle should be very slight, with the nose just a little higher than the rear of the saddle. Here again, however, the best test is feel, and most likely, you will want to make small seat adjustments from time to time during the break-in period.

What about the handlebars? The two factors here are your normal cycling position and arm length. If you have short arms or do not bend your body forward while pedaling, the goose-

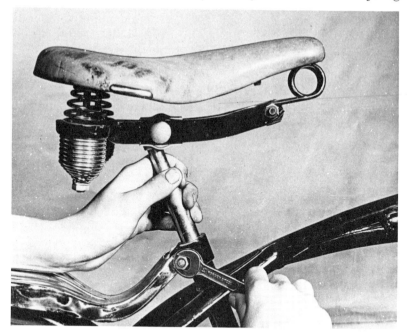

The clampnut for adjusting the seat level is at the top of the seat tube. The bolt for adjusting the seat angle can be seen in the clamp holding the seat to the seat post, above the boy's left index finger in this picture. Courtesy Boy Scouts of America

neck portion of the steering stem will probably be too long for you. This gooseneck length can be adjusted on some bikes. With others, you may need a different stem or handlebars. For normal cycling you should lean forward at least 10 degrees from vertical, and your hands should be able to grip the handlebars comfortably. If you have caliper brakes, the control levers must be within easy reach. This point must be checked carefully with children, whose hands are often too small to reach the levers. The only solution to this problem is a bike with coaster brakes.

Handlebar height and angle should feel right to you. Too much weight on the grips leads to sore arms and wrists. The recommended adjustment is to bring the top of the gooseneck to the same level as the nose of the saddle. To adjust the height, loosen the bolt at the top of the stem about half an inch. Then tap it down lightly. This frees an expansion nut within the stem. Now set the stem to the desired level and tighten the bolt, making sure the stem and front wheel are in line. You can change the angle of the handlebars simply by loosening the clamp nut at the end of the gooseneck.

Remember: in any adjustment, comfort and bike control are the most important considerations.

BIKE TYPES AND STYLES

To name the parts of a bike in the first chapter, we looked at just one type of bike. There are many other types, and the parts

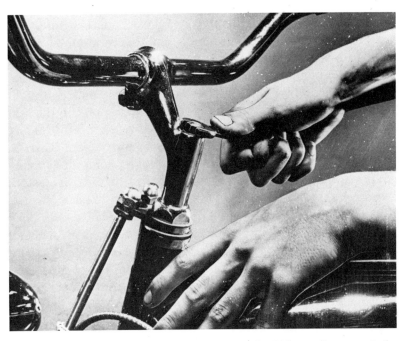

To adjust the handlebar height, unscrew the bolt at the top of the stem about half an inch and then tap down lightly to free the interior lock nut. The stem will now slide up or down. When retightening the bolt, be sure the stem gooseneck is aligned with the front wheel. You can adjust the handlebar angle by loosening the nut at the gooseneck clamp. Courtesy Boy Scouts of America vary greatly. In selecting a bike, you will have a wide choice of frame, seat, and handlebar styles. You also will have a choice of wheel and tire types. Gearing systems offer such a wide selection that we have devoted a special chapter to the subject. And accessories, which so often influence a beginner's judgment in selecting a bike, have also been given a chapter of their own.

Designers have tried to improve on the basic diamond pattern of the bicycle frame for several years. The results have ranged from interesting to ludicrous. Personally I do not think the standard design can be beaten for lightness and strength. But some of the variations do seem right, at least in appearance, for various bike styles. Two side-by-side top tubes that extend beyond the seat tube in a graceful curve to form the seat stays give a pleasing, low profile to many heavy-duty bikes.

The over and under top tubes with heavy, motorcycle-type tank as a filler, popular in prewar years, have fortunately all but vanished today. Girls' frames, usually with a double down tube to make up for the loss of the top tube, have attracted much attention from designers recently. The most interesting innovation is a tube or two side-by-side tubes angling straight from the top of the steering head to a midway point in the seat tube and then extending as stays to the rear-wheel drop-out. Such construction is often seen on frames for tandem bicycles.

Handlebars, particularly on novelty bikes, come in as many shapes as macaroni, but there are really just three basic designs —drop, level, and high-rise. Drop bars, which appear on most dérailleurs today, often bother beginners, because they look uncomfortable. You have to try drop bars to appreciate them. With hands on the grips and arms straight, your body comes forward about 45 degrees, an efficient angle for cycling. You not only get maximum leg power, but you also lower wind resistance. And the drop bar offers a variety of hand positions. You can sit back a bit and hold the bar with hands on either side of the gooseneck. You can lean forward and hold the bar halfway down at the bend sections, or you can hold the grips. Such changes of position can prevent sore hands and arms.

Flat handlebars usually are not perfectly flat but have a slight upward bend from the center. They are for cyclists who prefer leaning forward no more than about 10 degrees. Most veteran cyclists consider flat bars tiring, because of the limited choice of position. High-rise handlebars appear on most novelty bikes. Holding these bars brings the body slightly forward and the arms almost horizontal, a position high-rise advocates declare the most comfortable of all. For power cycling, however, the high-rise is no match for the drop bar.

There are three basic seat designs. The racing saddle, like the drop bar, looks uncomfortable and indeed takes some cyclists considerable use to appreciate. Narrow and hard, it should be regarded more as a prop than a true seat. The narrowness allows free leg movement, and the hardness prevents absorption of pedal power by cushions and springs. While your first few miles on a racing saddle may leave you feeling a little like an apple on a stick, this type of saddle is a must if your goals are speed, distance, or simply pedaling efficiency. The touring saddle is wide and softened by springs and cushions. It is ideal for the casual cyclist who does not like to put much weight on the handlebars. The banana seat, long and upholstered, is another novelty bike item. Its fore-and-aft dimension allows many positions and shifts of weight, ideal for the stunting cyclist.

Wheel styles are generally governed by tire type and size. The clincher tire, the ruggedest and most common, is composed of an inner tube and outer shell with beaded edges that fit snugly within the wheel rim. Wires imbedded within the beaded edge give the clincher tire its alternate name of "wired-on." The second tire type, the "sewn-on" or "sewn-up," is composed of a tube completely encircled by an outer shell that is sewn together at its inner face. This is an extremely light and responsive tire, used on nearly all racing bikes and some touring models. It also allows use of a lighter rim without the high edges needed to anchor the clincher tire. The sewn-on is harder to patch and less durable on rough ground. I don't recommend it for beginners.

Tires are measured by their width. Balloon tires are two or more inches wide. They provide good traction and can take a surprising amount of rough jolts on ruts, curbs, or rocky ground, but they also give much more road drag than the narrow, one- to one-and-a-quarter-inch tire. Wheel hubs, of course, vary with gear and brake systems, and quick-release skewers rather than conventional axle nuts are gaining popularity. The skewers speed up wheel removal, a real advantage if you have to change or repair a tire on the road. Racing bikes often have fewer than the standard thirty-six spokes, a reduction that cuts weight and wind resistance.

Brake designs are multiplying. There are two types of caliper brakes: center-pull and side-pull. The center-pull holds adjustment well and is slightly more efficient than the side-pull brake, but the center-pull is also more expensive. At the hub, the expansion brake, a drum-and-shoe arrangement patterned after the auto brake, is replacing the old stand-by coaster brake on some bikes. The greater braking surface of the expansion model makes it particularly useful on tandems. Some novelty bikes have appeared recently with sports-car-type disk brakes.

While pedal designs vary considerably, pedals can be separated into two distinct classes: rubber-grip pedals and all-metal or "rat trap" pedals. The rubber-grips have two bars of hard rubber held in a metal frame. The metal pedals, with toothed edges for improved grip, are often fitted with toe clips to increase efficiency.

If you are in the market for a geared bike, you should study the next chapter before making a decision. If the theory and mathematics of gearing do not interest you, then at least learn to recognize the various gearing systems. They fall into two classifications, those contained within the hub and those that employ a movable chain on various sizes of chain wheels and sprockets. The two-speed hub model is shifted through slight back-pedaling. The three- and five-speed hub models are controlled by cables leading to levers on the handlebars. The movable-chain, or dérailleur, system normally has five different-sized sprockets at the rear hub arranged like a cone, with the largest sprocket inside and the smallest outside. A cable and lever controls the chain carrier mechanism that positions the chain on the various sprockets. In a five-speed dérailleur there is just one chain wheel, but the ten-speeds have two chain wheels and the fifteen-speeds, three. The cage moving the chain to these various chain wheels is controlled by a second lever and cable. Chain wheels are arranged with the smallest inside and the largest outside.

The above description of various parts and systems suggests the possibility of an infinite number of bike types. Indeed, by changing parts and components, you can make your own bike a unique machine, but when you are shopping for a bike, you will find that they generally fall into five basic types. Let's discuss them one at a time.

BIKE TYPES

The beginners' bike, with a level handlebar, tourist seat, and single-gear, coaster-brake hub, is offered in a great range of sizes. Bike makers advertise their smallest models for riders two

The beginners' bike with removable training wheels is the best machine for learning, but you have to start early, because these models are for the very young. If you have outgrown a beginners' bike, you should learn the art of balancing by coasting down a gentle slope. Courtesy Schwinn Bicycle Company

to five years old. These normally have eight-inch frames and
sixteen-inch wheels. For older beginners, frame sizes of sixteen
to twenty inches and wheels from twenty to twenty-four inches
will be suitable. Beginners' bikes should have chain guards.
Most come with training wheels that can be removed when the
rider gains confidence. Wide tires, one and three quarters to
two inches, add to the stability of these bikes. Weight and
price vary with size. The smallest should weigh about twenty-
five, the largest close to forty pounds. With the exception of
some of the larger models, you should be able to buy a good
beginners' bike for less than fifty dollars.

In style and durability, the heavyweight bike is simply an
enlarged beginners' bike. Level handlebars, tourist seats, wide
tires, and coaster brakes are typical, with frames up to twenty-

*The heavyweight bike, really an enlargement of the beginners'
model, has a stout frame, fenders, wide tires, and single-speed hub.
Though it will not eat up the miles, the heavyweight is ideal for
delivery work and short trips to school or work.* Courtesy Schwinn
Bicycle Company

two inches and wheels up to twenty-six inches. Although it is
not the popular bike of prewar years, the heavyweight does
have remarkable durability. If geared, the hub will most com-
monly be the two-speed type that shifts by back pedal pressure. These bikes weigh as much as fifty pounds. You should be
able to buy a good one for fifty to sixty dollars. Cyclists with
swift dérailleurs often look on the heavyweights with disdain
and call them "trucks" or "steamrollers." The heavyweight does
have a place, however, and it would still be my choice if I were
back at my old job of delivering newspapers.

Novelty bikes are difficult to describe, and with new inno-
vations and designs coming from the factories each year, the

*The novelty bike appeared in the early 1960s, and its popularity has
grown steadily. The high-rise handlebars, banana seat, and small
wheels make this an ideal vehicle for stunting cyclists. This model
has a single-speed hub.* Courtesy Schwinn Bicycle Company

job gets more and more difficult. Generally, however, they are typified by high-rise handlebars, banana seats, and small, usually twenty-inch, wheel size. These cannot all be classed as children's bikes. Adults find them useful for short shopping trips or tours of the neighborhood. Many of the folding bikes offered today, which can be carried inside a car trunk, are novelty bikes. Frame size on these novelty jobs is misleading, because half the altitude is achieved through the high-rise bars and long seat posts. Strong riders get good acceleration with these small-wheeled bikes, and agile riders can lean back, pull the front wheel off the ground, and thus perform a "wheelie."

Novelty bikes can be found today with two- or three-speed hubs or five-speed dérailleur systems, and, of course, you can still find models with fixed gears. Weight ranges from thirty to forty pounds. Prices range from a low of sixty dollars for a fixed-speed to a hundred twenty dollars for the five-speed models. Some models, advertised with "stick shifts," "disk brakes," and "shocks," are designed for auto-oriented youth not yet old enough to drive. Novelty bikes can be great fun for tricks, short sprints, hill climbing, and bike rodeos. They are also dependable transportation for short trips, but don't attempt any long-distance touring with these small-wheelers. They will wear you out. Also, I recommend against this design for learners. They are not as stable as a conventional bike.

Utility bikes with level handlebars, tourist seats, caliper brakes, and conventional diamond-shaped frames are the most common European bike and have wide acceptance in America as well. They are sometimes misnamed the "English racer." They are not necessarily English and they are surely not racers. Some have a fixed-gear hub, but most on the market today have three- or five-speed hubs. The style is finding greater acceptance each year among young riders, so sizes vary. Adult models, however, have seventeen- to twenty-four-inch frames and twenty-six- or twenty-seven-inch wheels. One British company makes a utility bike with twenty-eight-inch wheels for the lanky cyclist. The most common tire width is one and three eighths inches. Utility bikes usually come with chain guards and fenders, and some have front and rear lights structured into the fenders. Some cyclists use utility bikes for touring or camping and swear by them, but their best use is for short jaunts, a visit to the park, a picnic in the country, shopping, or visiting in the neighborhood. Some manufacturers have started putting five- and ten-speed dérailleur systems on utility-style bikes, creating something of an off-breed machine. Utility bikes weigh in the neighborhood of thirty-five to forty pounds. Costs range from sixty dollars to over a hundred dollars, depending on the shifting system.

The lightweight bike, often referred to as a "ten-speed," has attracted the greatest attention in the current bicycle boom,

Some novelty bikes come with stick shift, shocks, drum expansion brakes in front, and disk brakes at the rear. This five-speed dérailleur model has a rear wheel bigger than the front. The features appeal to auto-oriented cyclists. Courtesy Schwinn Bicycle Company

The utility bike with tourist seat, level handlebars, and three-speed hub combines sturdy construction with increased range. Though not as easy to pedal as a lightweight, the utility bike is popular with touring cyclists in level country. This particular model, with a girls' frame, has twenty-six-inch wheels. Courtesy Schwinn Bicycle Company

and with good reason. With drop handlebars, racing seat, caliper brakes, rat-trap pedals, multiple-speed dérailleur system, and its lightness, this bike is designed to give the cyclist the best ride for his money. If you are in good shape, you can expect to cover a hundred miles in one day on such a machine. Lightweights can be a disappointment, however, if you forget that they are precision instruments designed for maximum efficiency. They are no good for hill-climbing contests, obstacle courses, or stunts. Rugged use will put them out of adjustment or perhaps cause expensive damage. The major criticism of the lightweight, in fact, is that it is too delicate. Some of the cheaper models do give owners problems, but a machine of reasonable quality, properly maintained, will give thousands

This five-speed bike cannot be classed as a lightweight, despite the dérailleur gearing system. The tourist seat, level handlebars, and chain guard put it closer to the utility class. Courtesy Schwinn Bicycle Company

of repair-free miles. A good machine should weigh little more than twenty-five pounds. Prices begin at eighty-five dollars and go up to five hundred dollars or more for custom-builts. All bikes, but particularly the lightweights, follow the adage of "you get what you pay for."

ODD TYPES

There are some off-breed bikes, some of which should be classed as "non-bikes." Unicycles and tricycles fall into this class. If you are agile and like the unusual, you can have great fun with a unicycle. Do not, however, look upon the unicycle

The lightweight bicycle is designed for maximum pedaling efficiency. The racing saddle, drop handlebars, and metal "rat-trap" pedals are distinguishing features of the lightweight. This model has toe clips, center-pull brakes, quick-release skewers, and a ten-speed dérailleur system. Note the absence of fenders. Very few of the high-priced lightweights have them. Courtesy Schwinn Bicycle Company

as transportation. It might get you to school and back if you live within walking distance, but the unicycle's best use is for stunts or parades. I have never learned to ride one, but young informants tell me there is a danger in the beginning of going backward when you want to go forward. The trick is to place the back side of the wheel against a timber before you mount. This gets you started in the right direction. Turning is the next difficulty. It is done entirely by changing balance. Some beginners carry a pole to aid in balance and to catch themselves to prevent serious spills.

Tricycles are offered for adults by most American manufacturers today. These can be extremely useful vehicles for elderly

An adult tricycle gives ideal transportation for community shopping trips or picnics in the park. The large cargo basket, putting the weight over the rear wheels, gives the tricycle real utility, and many adults, not confident on a two-wheeler, find the three-wheeler just right as an exerciser. Courtesy Schwinn Bicycle Company

cyclists who have given up regular bikes because of the threat of spills. Tricycles provide exercise and enough storage between the rear wheels to be practical cargo carriers. Tricycles with the double wheels in front get extensive use in Asia and South America. The pedicabs of the Far East, with the passenger sitting between the two front wheels and the "cabbie" pedaling furiously behind, are more common than motor-driven taxis in some cities.

Tandems come in many styles, from heavy-framed balloon-tired jobs to lightweights with ten-speed dérailleurs. I have found the heavy ones difficult to balance and steer, even dangerous for road use. The light models, however, are ideal for a husband-and-wife touring team, provided both are good cyclists. If one partner does all the work, the tandem becomes a drag.

Whether you are buying a new machine from a shop or a secondhand one from a stranger or a friend, there are some tests you should make for quality and condition. Even the best shops sometimes goof in assembling new bikes, and of course, a secondhand machine can have serious defects. First make sure all nuts and bolts are tightly seated. You can find rattles by lifting the bike by the handlebars and seat and bouncing it slightly on its tires. In addition, you should hand-test exposed nuts and bolts. Stripped threads in secondhand bikes are common.

Next spin the wheels to make sure they are true. If the wheel wobbles in the fork or stays, it could be due to unequal spoke tension or worn axle cones. If the spokes do not give pings of equal pitch as you run your fingers or a pencil across them, it means that some are looser than others and the wheel will have to be retuned. If you find lateral play by pulling and pushing at the rim, it means wear in the axle assembly or at least loose axle cones. Spin the wheel again to make sure it coasts to a stop. Actually, the weight of the stem valve alone at the three o'clock position should be enough to turn a properly adjusted wheel. Binding is usually due to tight cones or a dry axle.

Check the brakes. If they are caliper type, they should grab the rim evenly on both sides, and as you spin the wheel, the brakes should stop it without noise and without sticking. Make sure the shoes do not touch any portion of the tires. Coaster brakes should not grab at the first touch of back pressure on the pedals.

Check the pedals themselves. They should spin without wobble, and of course they should not bind.

Chains on coaster-brake or hub-geared bikes should not be too tight. A half inch of play in the chain is about right. On dérailleurs, chain tension is taken up by the springs of the chain carrier. On any kind of secondhand bike, it is best to remove the chain and check both the rear wheel and the bottom-bracket assembly for wobble. A tight chain can hide worn bearings. There should be very slight, preferably no, side play as you push and pull on the cranks.

With a secondhand bike, check the frame carefully for alignment and look for wrinkles and creases in the tubing, which would indicate an attempt to straighten a bent frame. Once a frame has been bent, realignment is difficult, and even if the frame does seem true, strength and resiliency can never

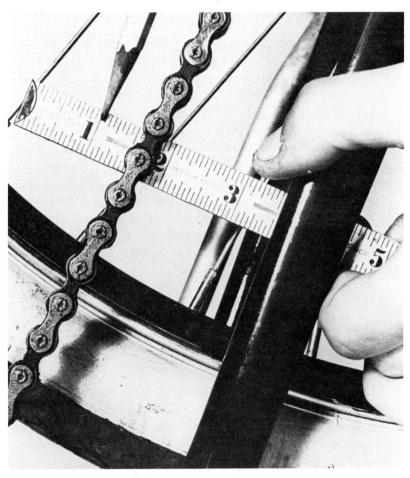

There should be no more than half an inch of play in the chain. A loose chain can be tightened by repositioning the wheel in the drop-out slots. When buying a used bike, beware of a tight chain. It can hide wheel wobble and worn bearings at the bottom bracket. Remove the chain to check for wear and wobble. Courtesy Boy Scouts of America

be restored to a damaged frame. Be particularly cautious of a recently repainted frame.

There are some brand names, particularly with dérailleurs, that you should learn. These bikes are made up of several components, and often, because of variable labor costs and different import fees between countries, you may find Italian gear components, French hubs, and English tubing on one bike.

For tubing, Reynolds 531 and Columbus rank at the top. Double-butted, rather than welded, joints give best strength and resilience. Butted joints have a double thickness of metal at the unions, while welded joints are smooth.

Top names in dérailleurs are Campagnolo, Shimano, Sun Tour, and Huret. Often these firms produce different grades of components. Campagnolo's Nuovo Record is top grade, Campagnolo's Record is second, and Campagnolo's Valentine rates third.

For the best hubs, look for Campagnolo and Normandy brand names; for pedals, Campagnolo and Lyotard. On crank sets, the best brands are Campagnolo, Stronglight, and Sugino. On brakes the best makers are Campagnolo, Universal, Mafac, and Weinmann.

Brand-name buying is an expensive way to shop for a bike, but it is also a sure way to get the best.

WHERE TO BUY

Large department stores and mail-order houses can beat the prices at bike shops by about 10–15 per cent. The saving, however, is debatable. Department stores rarely if ever have professional bicycle mechanics on their staffs, and bike assembly should be handled by a mechanic. The same reservation applies to bikes shipped directly to you by mail. If you are new at it, you may take a day getting the bike from packing case to well-adjusted assembly. And what if there is a defect or if something goes wrong with the new bike? The department store will have no expert to fix it, and shipping a bike back to a supplier takes both patience and effort. You might pay more at a bike shop, but the shop depends on satisfied customers. A good dealer will do his best to give you and your bike top service.

If you are buying a secondhand bike, do not let yourself be rushed. A common trick of the seller is to talk about all the other people he has lined up to buy the bike. Unfortunately few sellers will point out defects to you. You must look for them yourself. If you find something wrong, ask at a bike shop how much it will cost to fix. The seller should agree to deduct this from his asking price. If he refuses, let one of the "other people" buy the bike.

PRICES

There is a bike shortage in America, and makers and importers expect it to last a long time. All nine bicycle makers in this country rely to some degree on foreign components, and the foreign suppliers have not been able to fill orders promptly since 1971. The shortage has brought an unfortunate jump in prices. In some of the higher-priced dérailleurs, the prices have gone up more than 20 per cent over 1971 prices. Prices on less expensive models have taken 10–15 per cent jumps. In addition, some shop owners appear to ignore recommended prices. Why charge a hundred dollars for a bike when customers are eager to pay one twenty-five?

If you suspect a dealer of inflated prices, ask to see his price list. Check these against catalogue prices or prices on comparable models. As a general rule, well-established dealers will charge competitive prices, but until the current bicycle shortage is over, a little extra time checking prices can save you dollars.

4. Gears

Do gears confuse you? They shouldn't. The mathematics is basic, and the theory is no more complicated than the wheel itself.

Of course you do not have to understand gears in order to use them, but cycling will be more fun if you know what's going on in that linkage between your turning feet and the rear wheel of the bike. If you own or expect to own a dérailleur, gear knowledge is vital for efficient shifting and selection of gears.

The bicycle converts human effort into traveled distance. The cyclist wants to cover the most distance with the least work. If all roads led downhill, the desire could be easily met, but there are level roads and uphill roads. This is where gears come in handy.

As we have already seen, there are many kinds of bikes, some much more efficient than others. Weight, wind resistance, and road friction all work against the cyclist, but in comparing efficiency of bikes, the most significant measure is wheel size.

In one rotation, a large wheel travels farther than a small wheel. If the wheel diameter is known, you can figure the distance. For instance, a twenty-inch wheel travels 62.8 inches in one rotation. A twenty-seven-inch wheel travels 84.8 inches.

How do we know? The distance covered in one rotation is simply the circumference of a circle, and you figure circumference by multiplying the diameter by pi, or 3.14159. Use this formula on that giant, sixty-four-inch high-wheeler and you will find one revolution of the wheel would take that bike 201 inches, or nearly seventeen feet.

It would seem that the bigger the wheel the more efficient the bike. This, of course, was the conclusion reached by bicycle builders in the nineteenth century. But as we have already

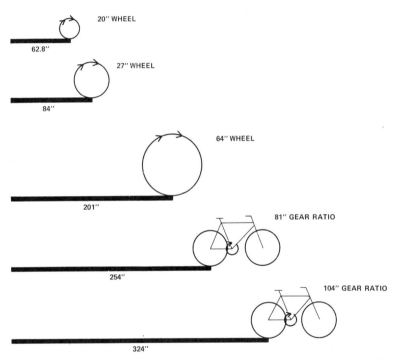

The bigger the wheel, the farther it travels in one revolution. The twenty-seven-inch wheel in the drawing above travels farther than the twenty-inch wheel, and the sixty-four-inch wheel travels farther than the twenty-seven-inch wheel. With gears, however, the twenty-seven-inch wheel can be made more efficient: one turn of the chain wheel will send a bike farther than the distance covered by the sixty-four-inch wheel, and a modern dérailleur in its top gear can go farther yet on one turn of the chain wheel. Gear ratios for bikes, given in inches, represent the diameters of hypothetical wheels.

seen, those high-wheeled monsters, though fast on the level, took almost superhuman effort to start and had to be pushed, dragged, or carried uphill. Smaller wheels might not cover as much distance, but they take less effort to turn. In other words, a small-wheeled bike would serve best for hill climbing, while a large-wheeled bike would serve best for level travel.

To illustrate this further, let's imagine three hypothetical bikes all following the old high-wheeler design with pedal cranks linked directly to the front axles. The first has a twenty-inch wheel, the second a twenty-seven-inch wheel, and the third a sixty-four-inch wheel. A man on the smallest bike would have to pedal faster than a man on the twenty-seven-inch bike to keep pace, and against the biggest bike, the man on the twenty-incher would have to pedal at an exhausting rate. His feet would be a blur, while the feet of the man on the sixty-four-incher would turn at a leisurely rate. Soon after these three bikes reached a hill, however, the sixty-four-incher would stop. The twenty-seven-incher might continue until the grade grew steep, while the twenty-incher would continue to the top.

Now let's talk about modern bikes, which, instead of direct drive to the axle, have chain wheels. Your inexpensive, single-speed bike actually has gears. The chain wheel is a gear, and the rear sprocket is a gear. When you know the size of these two gears, you can figure the efficiency of the gear drive. Sizes of gears are found by counting the teeth.

If you have ever looked inside a watch, you know that a small gear set at the edge of a large one turns much faster than the large gear. If the circumference of the small one is, say, one third that of the large one, then the small gear turns three times as fast.

If the chain sprocket of a bike has forty-eight teeth and drives a rear sprocket of sixteen teeth, then the rear sprocket will turn three times for each turn of the chain sprocket. You get this by dividing the tooth count on the rear sprocket into the count on the chain sprocket.

Now suppose this particular bike has twenty-seven-inch wheels. One turn of the chain sprocket will drive the rear wheel of the bike through three revolutions. We already know that this wheel covers 84.8 inches with one revolution. In three revolutions it would cover 254.4 inches, or slightly more than twenty-one feet. That is a greater distance than a man with a sixty-four-inch high-wheeler could manage with one turn of his pedals. In effect, the gears have increased the diameter of the wheel three times. The twenty-seven-inch wheel thus does the work of an eighty-one-inch wheel.

Here we have the key to bicycle gearing. Suppose, instead of sixteen teeth on the rear sprocket, there are twenty-four. Twenty-four divided into the forty-eight-tooth count of the chain sprocket gives two, and two times the twenty-seven-inch wheel would give fifty-four inches. A bike with this setup would travel 169.6 inches ($54 \times$ pi), or slightly more than fourteen feet, for each turn of the pedals. The "fifty-four-inch wheel," while not as efficient for level pedaling, would be better for climbing than the eighty-one-inch wheel.

Cyclists refer to these "wheel" sizes resulting from various gear combinations as gear ratios. As we have seen, you must know the tooth count for the chain sprocket and the rear sprocket as well as the bike's wheel diameter to figure ratios. The formula looks like this:

$$\text{Gear ratio} = \frac{\text{chain-sprocket teeth}}{\text{rear-sprocket teeth}} \times \text{wheel diameter.}$$

Since the gear ratio is actually the measure in inches of a hypothetical wheel diameter, you simply multiply it by pi to find the distance traveled for each turn of the pedals.

As you can see, the gear ratio is relatively easy to determine on a single-speed bike. Bikes with two-speed hubs that are shifted by back pedal pressure are a little more difficult to rate by gear ratio, because the hub gears are described by percentage. The two most common two-speed hubs on American bikes are made by Bendix. The hub with a yellow stripe has a 32 per cent reduction gear. Thus if your normal gear ratio, figured from tooth count and wheel size, is 60, the low gear with one of these hubs would be 32 per cent less, or 41.

The other Bendix two-speed hub, identified by three blue

belts, has a 47 per cent overdrive. If your normal gear ratio is 60, shifting will give you a 47 per cent increase, or a gear ratio of 88.

Three-speed hubs, of course, give you a wider range of gear ratios. Take a bike with twenty-six-inch wheels, a forty-four-tooth chain sprocket, and an eighteen-tooth rear sprocket. With the average three-speed hub, you would get a low of 48, a normal of 64, and a high of 85. A three-speed hub on a bike with twenty-six-inch wheels, a fifty-tooth chain sprocket, and a sixteen-tooth rear sprocket would give a gear-ratio spread of 61, 81, and 108, ideal for flat-country touring. The same hub on a twenty-six-inch-wheel bike with a forty-tooth chain sprocket and a twenty-tooth hub would give a spread of 39, 52, and 69, good ratios for hills. Thus, while a three-speed hub is an improvement over two-speed and fixed speeds, it still does not give a gear-ratio spread that will suit all kinds of travel, at least not without changing chain-sprocket and rear-sprocket sizes.

If one could change chain- and wheel-sprocket sizes, then . . .

It was this very thought that led Velocio to invent the dérailleur system. This is precisely what you do with a dérailleur when you shift. You move your chain to sprockets of different sizes. Here you can achieve the range in gear ratios that will suit all terrain.

Actually, with sprockets all out in the open, a dérailleur bike offers the best illustration for the principles of gearing we have been discussing in this chapter. Let's look at a typical ten-speed, a twenty-seven-inch-wheel model with gear ratios ranging from 32 to 104, a far bigger spread than any possible on a bike with a three-speed hub. The five wheel sprockets on this bike have fourteen, seventeen, twenty-two, twenty-eight, and thirty-four teeth respectively. The small chain sprocket has forty teeth and the large fifty-four teeth. Using the gear-ratio formula, you can calculate the result of all possible gear combinations, and you can figure the distance each combination would give you with one turn of the pedals. In tabular form, the results would look like this:

Wheel sprocket					
Chain sprocket	34	28	22	17	14
40	32	39	49	63	77
distance	8.4'	10.2'	12.8'	16.4'	20'
54	43	52	66	86	104
distance	11.2'	13.6'	17.3'	22.5'	27.2'

If you have just acquired a dérailleur, it might be a good idea to make out a chart for your gear combinations and tape it to the handlebars. With a little practice, you will learn the feel of the various gear ratios. In practical application you will notice at once that the lowest ratio is reached when the chain is closest to the centerline of the bike and the highest ratio when the chain has been moved to its outermost limits, but you should learn to shift without straining your neck to look down at the chain.

It takes practice to use a dérailleur bike effectively, and abuse can cause costly damage. The chain wheel must be turning when you change gears. The chain rides from one sprocket to another only if it is moving, but if you shift with too much strain on the chain, you can force it between sprockets, lock your wheel, and possibly break the chain or bend your sprockets. This means that if you are approaching a hill, you should shift down before you are putting great force on the pedals. At the other extreme, you should not shift down too early. Unless you speed up your rate of pedaling, you will lose speed before you reach the hill. Experienced cyclists rarely change their rate of pedaling. They keep the pedals turning at the cadence that suits them and adjust their gears according to terrain. A steady cadence prevents fatigue in long-distance touring or racing. You should decide what cadence suits you best and then try to stick to it. Once you know your pedaling cadence, you can work out your speeds for each gear ratio on your bike. This can be a great help in planning a trip.

For instance, if you pedal at ninety turns to the minute and your lowest gear ratio is 32, you can figure on traveling 720 feet per minute, which works out to 8.2 miles per hour. If your top gear ratio is 104, the same cadence will take you

2,430 feet in one minute, or 27.6 miles per hour. Of course, in actual practice, you will not get these rates, because wind resistance will always work against you.

Many veteran cyclists do not want as wide a range of gear ratios as the 32–104 example given here. This is particularly true of European cyclists who do not have the steep hills that American cyclists have. This is important when buying a foreign bike. Find out what the range of gear ratios is. If it does not suit you, ask for a different set of sprockets. You may have to wait for the new parts to be delivered, but it will be worth the trouble. The gears on your dérailleur should fit your ability and take you where you want to go.

5. Accessories

Bicycle accessories add weight. They increase wind resistance. The fewer accessories you put on your bike, the happier you will be. The only exception to this rule is when the accessory contributes to safe cycling.

In a bike shop, the heavy head lamp, the chrome fenders, the horn, and the big front carrying basket dazzle the customer. Such extras have clinched many sales and will continue to do so. Manufacturers will continue to produce overburdened bikes. But consider the typical history of such accessories.

Unfortunately the head lamp is usually the first piece of equipment to be shed. Probably the batteries have just started to corrode when the bike owner decides to do without the lamp. If he does any night cycling, this is a dangerous and, in some states, illegal decision. But what good is a lamp with corroded batteries? Soon after its novelty has worn off, the horn will be removed from the bike. The owner has discovered that a good healthy shout is more effective than most horns, and that horns in general are difficult to use in time of emergency, because at these times you need both hands firmly on the grips of your handlebars. That front basket, which the bike salesman said would hold a day's supply of groceries, will be shed next. The salesman neglected to explain how all that weight over the front wheel changes the balance and upsets the stability of a bike. Fenders may survive the shedding season for several months. They do help the cyclist stay clean on wet streets and mud, but they also have a way of developing rattles. If the bike owner is not too fastidious, the fenders will soon join the head lamp, horn, and basket in the darkest corner of the garage.

This shedding process is really too typical to be funny. Take a long, hard look at accessories.

What do you need on a bicycle? It depends, again, on the type of cycling you plan to do. If you travel at night, you must have lights. If you go camping, you will want sensible racks and carrying bags. If you go on rural tours, you will probably want to carry a water bottle, a tool kit, and an air pump. Don't buy accessories for their appearance. Buy them for their practical use. Let's consider them here by use.

FOR SAFETY

There are so many lamps on the market that selection is difficult. You want one big and bright enough to be seen for at least five hundred feet. While it should illuminate the road surface so you can avoid ruts or broken glass, the lamp's main purpose is to let others see you. You can buy a battery-powered model or a generator system. With battery lamps, you can remove the batteries for daytime cycling, to reduce weight. Some battery lamps can be slipped onto brackets as needed, and you can get lamps with rechargeable batteries. The generator lighting system is far more difficult to remove and repair. Most of these systems include a tail lamp—a good supplement for reflectors. Some cyclists say the generator produces excessive drag when running off the wheel of the bike. The worst thing to be said about the generator system is that it is always with you, adding weight whether you need it or not. My preference for occasional night riding is an ordinary flashlight with a light bracket. The flash slips easily in and out of the bracket, and it is a simple thing to remove the bracket itself. On camping trips, the flash serves double duty as a utility light, and, during the day, it can be stowed in your pack, out of sight of petty thieves.

Most rear fenders have built-in reflectors. On bikes without fenders, reflectors can be mounted on brackets at the axle, chain or seat stays, seat post, or the seat itself. Some states require pedal reflectors on all bikes sold. These are ideal, because the up-and-down motion attracts attention, but they must be considered as supplements to fixed reflectors. Pedal reflectors, by the way, do little good when covered with mud or road dust. Keep your pedals clean.

Reflective tape is one of the best safety buys you can make, and it adds negligible weight. You can buy it in many colors, but white tape not only shows up well at night but also catches light well on shaded streets during the day.

You should wear light-colored clothing at night, preferably white. You can also buy reflectorized jackets, vests, and belts. The triangular "fanny bumper," which hangs from the belt, is ideal. Some bike clubs supply these to all their members for both day and night use. In addition to bright or reflectorized clothing, you can also wear lights strapped to your arms or legs. These lights throw an amber beam front and back. Though you cannot use them in lieu of a head lamp, the strap lights provide excellent protection. Strapped to a leg, they give an up-and-down motion that is bound to be seen.

Are horns and bells worth the weight and money? Most cyclists say no, and some even argue that horns contribute to a dangerous cycling philosophy. A safe cyclist does not get into a situation where a horn is needed. Besides, against traffic noise, nearly all horns sound pitifully weak. The only exception is a Freon horn, modeled after the yachtsman's fog warning. This pressure-can device will stop traffic a block ahead and send pedestrians up lampposts. It is so loud, in fact, that you must use it cautiously.

Rearview mirrors mounted on handlebars can be a nuisance and are easily broken. How about mounting them on your head? No fooling! It's being done. In fact, the best rearview mirror on the market today is designed to clip to the visor of a cap or the temple bow of eyeglasses. Light and easy to stow, these small mirrors give adequate warning of overtaking traffic. Many modern cars make little noise; you do not always hear them approach. The small mirrors are the answer.

While most cyclists believe accidents and spills will happen to the other fellow, a crash helmet makes sense for safe cycling. You can use the conventional racing helmet of padded strips, or you can buy caps with built-in protection. Remember, broken arms and legs will mend, but you may never recover from a cracked head. A dedicated woman cyclist I know suffered concussion when her bike hit a rut and spilled her. It took her six months to recover, and she has not been cycling since. Unfortunately women are particularly reluctant to wear crash helmets.

Before leaving safety, there is one accessory I want to advise against—namely, bike radios. Hearing is as important as sight for safe cycling. Radios mask out sounds. Besides, it seems to me that a cyclist with a radio misses one of the great pleasures of rural bike riding. That is traveling in silence. It is such a rare pleasure that it seems a pity to miss it.

FOR PEACE OF MIND

To discourage thieves, you must carry a stout padlock and a case-hardened chain with links made of steel three eighths inch in diameter. A five-foot length of such chain runs about thirteen dollars. A lock with hardened shackle that is not easy to pick will cost about ten dollars. The chain and lock weigh about eight pounds. I would like to recommend a cheaper and lighter combination, but I cannot. Lighter stuff is practically an invitation to the professional bike thief. It can be cut with clippers that the thief can hide in his pocket. The heavier gear will at least force him to carry bolt cutters or expend a considerable amount of energy and time with a hack saw. Unfortunately nothing yet invented will stop a determined thief.

When locking your bike, pass the chain through the frame and at least one wheel, and then loop the chain around a tree, a post at least ten feet high, or something else that the locked bike cannot be lifted from. Some cyclists carry two padlocks and make double loops in their chains, forcing the thief to cut the chain twice. An old bike inner tube, incidentally, makes a good protective sleeve for a chain.

When you are touring far from the repair shop, tools and spare parts can add to your peace of mind. You should read chapter 10 on emergency road repair before you decide what to carry on your bike. It would be silly, for instance, to carry spare chain links if you have not the tool or the know-how to replace links. Most touring cyclists carry a tire patch kit and an air pump. Although I have used spoon handles to remove a tire, it is best to carry the tire tools built for the job. You should also have a pair of pliers, a screwdriver, an adjustable wrench, and a multijawed wrench made specially for cyclists. Even if you are taking just a one-day tour, I recommend carrying a

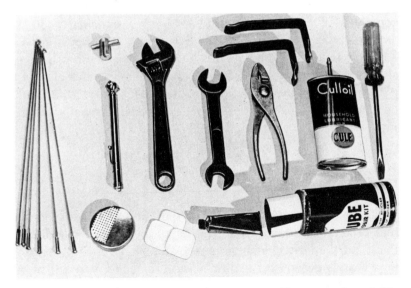

For repairs on the road, you will want a well-equipped tool kit. Spare spokes are at left. Valve gauge is just right of the spare spokes, and spoke wrench is just above the valve gauge. Notice the perforated disk at the bottom of the photo, just left of the spokes. It is for roughing rubber before applying rubber cement and a tube patch. Tire irons are above pliers in this photo. Not pictured here is a portable air pump, which would be needed for any tire repair work. Courtesy Boy Scouts of America can of light oil in the tool kit. Light air pumps with brackets to hold them on the top tube or the seat tube are relatively inexpensive and can make the difference in getting you home before dark.

Spare parts are a matter of individual choice and the nature of your trip. If you will be traveling over rough roads, spare spokes and an extra inner tube might be needed to keep you rolling. You will need a special wrench to replace spokes properly. I was saved from a long walk once, when a well-equipped friend produced a spare valve stem to replace my worn one. Now I carry spares in my own kit. Experiences such as this are the best guide in selecting tools and parts for travel. When touring with a group, it is unnecessary for everyone to carry air pumps, tire irons, and heavy wrenches. Portion such gear out so that no one is overburdened.

Cyclometers that fit on your hub and tick up the mileage come under the peace-of-mind category, particularly on an unfamiliar route. How far you have gone and how far you have yet to go to reach your planned stop determine your pace and let you know well before dusk if you should make alternate plans. Knowing your mileage also helps if you are training or on some kind of exercise program. And it is personally satisfying.

FOR COMFORT

Water bottles, the plastic kind that fit in brackets on the seat tube or the down tube, can keep you from a maddening thirst, particularly during summer weather. Even if you rarely take liquids except at mealtimes in normal life, you will want to drink when cycling. Perspiration builds thirst quickly. Some cyclists carry fruit juice instead of water, but a sweetened juice can sometimes stimulate rather than slake thirst.

Clothing, difficult to classify as a bicycle accessory, will be discussed in a later chapter. Just remember that cycling is a body-warming exercise. You might be cold in a light jersey and shorts while you are standing around, but once you start pedaling, such an outfit can be just the right thing.

FOR CARGO

Bike shops offer a wide selection of baskets, racks, cases, and bags for carrying cargo. Make your choice carefully. Light, rear racks with waterproof saddlebags are ideal for camping. They keep the center of gravity low and over the rear wheel, where it should be. Wire baskets serve well for shopping trips, but they are pesky things to remove when you don't need them. Big front baskets can be dangerous when fully loaded.

You can buy seats for carrying infants on a bike. You should always mount these behind your seat, and make sure the one you buy has guards to keep small feet out of spokes. Personally I consider even the best of these seats dangerous. An infant is helpless and exposed in a spill.

Cargo trailers have answered the need for campers who want more gear than they can carry comfortably on a bike. Do not buy a cheap one that doesn't track well. A wobbling trailer on a downgrade can cause a bad spill. Even the best of these two-wheeled jobs have the disadvantage on road travel of keeping you from staying on the extreme right, and that left wheel will worry you and passing motorists.

FOR NOVELTY

Many accessories must be classed as toys or novelties. Unless you recognize them as such, they will be disappointing. For instance, if you must know how fast you are going at any moment, buy a speedometer. If you want to attract attention, buy tassels, banners, and windmills. They can be fun for a parade, but they can make normal cycling hard work. I think such decorations are out of place on a good touring machine, but you are entitled to your own opinion.

How about motors on bikes? Here I may really show my bias. It is sufficient to say that if you put one of these noisy, one-cylinder motors on your machine, you no longer have a bicycle. It is a motor bike, and you may be required to get a special license to operate it.

PART II
Using Your Bike

6.   Safety Rules and Habits

If all cyclists obeyed the law and avoided risk, the annual toll from bicycle accidents, instead of increasing steadily each year, would take a dramatic drop. Unfortunately, intensive training programs and stricter law enforcement have so far not reversed the tragic rise in injuries and deaths.

The forty thousand injuries resulting from collisions between bicycles and motor vehicles in 1971 represent a ten-year increase of 47 per cent, while the death total of 850 for 1971 represents a 73 per cent increase over the same period. These figures from the National Safety Council have just one good feature: 'The increases have been slightly under the increase in cycling population during the same decade. But this can hardly be much consolation for the victims, and some states where year-round cycling is possible have mounting accident tolls far out of proportion to the rest of the nation.'

In California, for instance, bike accidents in 1971 rose 34.1 per cent over the previous year, and the state Highway Patrol office expects cycling fatalities to exceed pedestrian fatalities by 1975.

In analyzing its statistics the National Safety Council found that 80 per cent of the cyclists killed or injured were violating the law at the time of the accident and that 20 per cent of the bicycles involved had mechanical defects.

Common violations listed by the council were:

1. Using the middle of the street.
2. Failing to yield the right of way.
3. Riding too fast for traffic or road-surface conditions.
4. Ignoring traffic signs or signals.
5. Going against the flow of traffic.
6. Improper turning.

Who has the accidents? This is perhaps the most revealing fact to come from the council's figures. Most of those killed or injured were from five to fourteen years old. A breakdown of the figures for 1968, when thirty-eight thousand cyclists were injured, shows that twenty-nine thousand, or 76 per cent, were in this age bracket. Of the eight hundred deaths for the year, five hundred, or 62 per cent, were from five to fourteen years old. This age group, the council concluded, has the poorest knowledge of the law, the least experience, and the greatest collection of risky riders. Cyclists under fourteen also use their bikes for races and games more than older riders. When these games are held in the streets, accidents occur. This group obviously has the most to learn in terms of safety rules and habits.

THE LAW

Traffic laws are based on common sense. Cyclists, just like motorists, must follow the laws. The bicycle is a vehicle. A policeman can cite you for violations.

As the operator of a vehicle, you must ride on the right side of the road, with the flow of traffic. It is true that pedestrians walk against the flow of traffic, but on a bike you are not a pedestrian. There are several common-sense reasons for staying on the right side. For one thing, you have a better chance, moving with the traffic, to observe conditions as they develop ahead of you. Also, the motorist overtaking you has more time to observe and avoid you.

As the operator of a vehicle, you must observe the rules of traffic right of way. At an intersection the vehicle on your right may cross first unless there are signs or lights directing otherwise. A cyclist does not have the right to decrease the normal speed of traffic. If cars are unable to pass, and start backing up behind you, you should pull off and stop to let them pass. You must not pedal out of side streets without stopping to check for cars and pedestrians.

As the operator of a vehicle, you are obliged to signal your turns. In most states, the left arm held up means a right turn; straight out, a left turn; and down, a stop. Check, if you have caliper brakes, to make sure the right hand grip leads to the rear brake. This is important when signaling, because your right hand remains on the handlebars, and only the rear brake should be applied alone. Never use the front brake without using the rear at the same time.

As the operator of a vehicle, you must give pedestrians the right of way. Sidewalks, unless local laws say otherwise, are for pedestrians. If you must use a busy sidewalk, get off your bike and push it.

As the operator of a vehicle, you are not allowed to swerve or weave unsafely. If you lack the skill to ride in a straight line, you have no business in traffic. Practice until you have full control of your bike.

As the operator of a vehicle, you must never drive at night without a head lamp and a rear reflector. That is the minimum. Some states and cities are sensibly requiring more.

In addition to general rules regulating vehicles, there are some special rules for cyclists:

You should never hitch a ride by holding onto another moving vehicle.

You should never carry a passenger or cargo on your bike in such a way that he, she, or it restricts vision or upsets balance. In some states it is illegal to carry a passenger on your handlebars.

You should not modify your bike at the expense of control and stability. Some states require that the low pedal be no more than one foot from the ground and that high-rise handlebars with grips higher than the head be banned.

You should never ride your bike on freeways, turnpikes, or other thoroughfares where bicycles are specifically forbidden.

Following the law, of course, will not make you immune from accidents. You can be within your rights and still be hurt. Unfortunately there always will be dangerous drivers and faulty streets. A cyclist has poor protection. You should not dispute the right of way with a motorist even when you are right.

Let caution become a habit. Here are some ways to practice caution in city traffic:

At a crowded intersection, if you plan a left turn, get off your bike and use the crosswalk with the pedestrians. Even if you have special turn signals in your favor, left turns are one of the most dangerous maneuvers in city traffic.

When passing parked cars, be alert for motorists getting out. A door swung open in your path can cause a serious crash. Yes, the motorist is supposed to look behind him before opening the door, but most look only if they hear a car. They do not expect a bike, and you do not make enough noise to warn them.

Beware of other cyclists, particularly the very young ones. These are the unpredictable pedalers. Sometimes one wonders if they themselves know where they will turn next.

Bridge expansion joints and drain gratings pose a special threat for the cyclist. If you drop a wheel into one of these hazards, you can be seriously hurt. Your bike can be badly damaged. Little can be done about bridge expansion joints except dismounting from your bike and walking across. Trying to swerve to cross them at an angle is chancy, and doing that in traffic is outright dangerous. Drain gratings running with the flow of traffic can be reported to the city's public works department. The city might not change its grates, but it may buy sensible ones in the future.

Needless to say, the city street is not the place to practice tricks and stunts. Cycling with no hands has brought grief to many cyclists. Unless you are signaling, you need both hands on the handlebars. Your attention must be on the traffic. Safe bike riders think ahead, anticipating traffic situations before they develop. They do not let themselves become caught against the curb by a right-turning vehicle. They see the car in the side road before it pulls into their path. They stay well clear of a backing motorist. All this takes concentration. You cannot concentrate when you are performing stunts.

If possible, plan your trips to avoid rush hours. At least study a map long enough before you start to find the best route to your destination. Often a detour of a few blocks will take you away from the worst of city traffic.

Here are some special points of caution for country cycling:

Rural intersections frequently are unmarked, and even when cross traffic must stop, motorists may not see you. Despite the cycling boom, motorists in many parts of rural America do not expect to see bicycles. Often shrubs and trees cut visibility at curves as well as intersections. Take these sections of the road slowly.

You will probably travel faster on country roads than in city traffic. This means you must be especially alert for rocks and broken glass. If you do not see these hazards in time to avoid them, it means you are traveling too fast. It may also mean that you will have a flat tire.

When cycling in a group, travel single file, as far to the right as possible, with a space of at least four bike lengths between you and the fellow ahead. If you don't maintain spacing, one man's spill can turn into a sudden convention.

Slow down and avoid sharp turns on dirt, sand, or gravel. Often, loose material collects at the side of the road where you are required to travel. You must concentrate on the surface ahead and slow down before the trouble spot.

Know your route before you start. Carry a map if you are not sure you can remember the route, and do not try to cover so many miles in one day that you exhaust yourself. The safety factor diminishes rapidly as you tire.

Dogs pose a special problem for cyclists. In most cities dog owners are supposed to keep their animals under control, but in the country dogs run free. Bites can be serious enough, but, in addition to that, you suffer the danger of rabies. It never is easy after a bite to locate the owner of a dog in the country. For one thing, the dog is still around, threatening, and you are hurting. Just the same, you must have information on the dog: when, if ever, it was last vaccinated against rabies and who will take responsibility for observing the dog if it has not been vaccinated. Usually the county health officer has jurisdiction. In addition to all this, you must have the bite treated. Dog bites are particularly subject to infection. Most doctors will help you in reporting bites to health officers and in trying to locate dog owners.

Naturally you will want to avoid being bitten in the first place. The best way is simply to outdistance the dog. You can usually do it on level ground. I have known cyclists who carry a short whip with a quick-release strap on a tube of their bike frame. A smart crack across a dog's nose usually discourages it from pursuit. Other cyclists carry special dog repellent in pressure cans. Personally I am always too busy pedaling away from the dog to think about whips and sprays, but such devices might be effective, particularly with dogs that have become habitual troublemakers. Don't think from this that city dogs cannot cause trouble, but, in the city, owners are more conscious of their responsibility or at least can be quickly made conscious if you complain.

What about cycling in bad weather? Ice, even soggy leaves, will spill you abruptly. Wet streets are not quite as dangerous, but that first rain after a long dry spell often leaves a treacherous film on the pavement. Wet leaves in the fall are a further hazard. Snow over three inches deep is too deep for cycling, and remember, the snow can hide a film of ice. What all this means is that bad-weather cycling comes down to personal judgment, provided it is good judgment. Visibility is reduced in rain, snow, or fog; and of course the pavement will be slick. Winds may upset your balance. If you are aware of all these extra hazards and still want to venture forth, then go to it.

SAFETY PROGRAMS

Judging from statistics, membership in a bicycle club is the best move anyone can make toward safe cycling. Club members have very few accidents. Why? Usually cyclists do not join clubs until they have had some experience, but this is not the entire reason for their "clean" record. Most clubs give new members a thorough briefing in safety, and all members take pride in their bikes, their skill, and their record.

Safety is a common topic at club meetings. Safety films and printed information are nearly always available through clubs. Some clubs, as we have already seen, distribute safety accessories such as "fanny bumpers" to their members, and club jerseys are either of bright colors or incorporate bright colors in their pattern.

In addition to the work of clubs, many police departments today offer bicycle safety programs and conduct checks for bicycle defects. This is usually coupled with a stepped-up program of enforcement.

Marin County, on the north side of San Francisco Bay, was hard hit by the bicycle boom and hard pressed to develop an accident-prevention program. "This thing hit us overnight," said Highway Patrol Officer Keith E. Chapman in a recent interview. Chapman, put in charge of the problem in Marin County, developed a one-day inspection and demonstration session for schools. He calls it the "Stop-on-a-dime" program, and the point is that no one, whether motorist, cyclist, runner, or walker can stop on a dime. First of all, it takes reaction time from the moment your ears hear or your eyes see danger, for your brain to signal the body. A cyclist going twenty miles an hour travels fifteen feet during this reaction time, and it takes another twenty-one feet to bring the bike to a stop. These distances, and the even greater distances for autos, are related to crosswalks and intersections. Young cyclists appreciate at once the dangers of recklessness in traffic.

Chapman's program has worked well, but there is one group he has not yet been able to reach in his educational effort: the parents. "Too many parents work with a child only long enough to see that he can balance the bike. Then they say, 'Okay, son, the world is yours.' All too often," Chapman continued, "we stop a child on the wrong side of the road only to hear, 'This is how my dad told me to ride.'"

Perhaps Marin's new citation system for cycling violations with a central office mailing copies of citations home to parents of cyclists fifteen years and under will help educate the group Officer Chapman has so far failed to reach.

A bicycle test lane with rollers under both wheels provides an ideal test for braking speed and efficiency. The testing officer can also check for wheel wobble and give a close visual check of all parts of the bike. If the bike does not fit the cyclist or if the cyclist lacks confidence, it becomes quickly apparent on a test lane. Courtesy California State Automobile Association

In addition to the work of local police, there are concerned
national organizations that offer training courses, films, pamphlets, and suggestions for safety-training sessions in schools.
The National Safety Council has recently compiled a training

*Reflective tape on fenders and frame of a bike is an excellent in-
vestment for safety. Here a police officer with a volunteer member
of the Veterans of Foreign Wars help a young cyclist apply the
tape.* Courtesy California State Automobile Association

course called "All About Bikes," which schools can purchase at a nominal fee per pupil. You can receive information by writing to the council at 425 North Michigan Avenue, Chicago, Illinois 60611.

The Bicycle Institute of America publishes safety pamphlets and has several films that can be borrowed without charge. Write the institute at 122 East 42nd Street, New York, N.Y. 10017.

State offices of the American Automobile Association provide training material on bike safety. You can have information by calling or writing the office nearest you.

As you can see, there are certainly enough individuals and organizations working for safer cycling, but there is one person who can do more than anyone else to make the bike safer. That person is you.

7. Touring

Your bike can take you to and from school or a job. It can take you through your neighborhood, and it can introduce you to parks and points of scenic or historic interest. It can put you in competition, either in serious racing or in games. It can do all these things and more, but one of the greatest cycling pleasures is touring. Certainly, judging from the growing numbers of bikes on rural roads today, touring has become the most popular of all cycling activities.

What is touring? It can range from a jaunt of a few hours to several weeks of hard travel. It can be a brief expedition into farm lands near home or it can take you to foreign countries. You can pedal leisurely along the routes where soldiers of the American Revolution marched, or you can puff vigorously up slopes that lead you into the shadows of a snow-capped western peak. Touring is hard to define, but the key word seems to be "planning." You plan your trip, where you will go, what you will see, who will go with you, how much you will carry, and where you will eat and sleep along the way. Of course this can be as organized or as informal as you wish, but, when touring, you will want to follow some sort of plan. For most touring cyclists, planning a trip is half the fun.

WHO WILL GO

This can be one of the most difficult parts of tour planning. You can have a close friend who makes a fine companion on the playing field or in school but is no good as a cycling companion. Sometimes it's because he or she is not a good cyclist and cannot keep up with others. Often it's temperament: The friend loses interest in what you want to do and starts an argument by suggesting or even following alternate plans. Of course, selection of traveling companions is particularly important on tours of several days, but one troublemaker can practically ruin a day trip, too.

Members of your group should have similar abilities and equipment. Don't expect the three-speed cyclists to keep up with the ten-speed tourers. One solution with a mixed group is to divide the cyclists by ability or bikes at the beginning, and start the slow group early. Or, if your tour follows a loop, you can often designate short cuts for the slower cyclists. This way, everyone can reach the destination at about the same time, and while the fast cyclists may have seen more country, no one is exhausted at the end of the day.

Unless the tour is sponsored and organized by a bike club or some other group, you and your companions should get together well in advance of the trip, discuss the route, decide how much time will be devoted to side trips or sight-seeing, agree on sharing expenses, and, as already mentioned, make sure that tools and spare parts will be equally distributed. You might also want to appoint a leader.

The need for a leader depends a great deal on the nature of your group. Most adult cyclists appoint a leader to check the route before the tour, see to restaurants and night accommodations, and make reservations if necessary. The assignment of leader often changes with each tour, thus spreading the responsibility. With younger cyclists the leadership issue sometimes gets touchy. As you know, this problem is not limited to bicycle touring; it's one of life's problems. In any case, if you decide on a tour leader, he or she should understand what the job means and know how much help the rest of you can give in planning. In the beginning, I recommend that your leader be an experienced cyclist who knows what too many hills, too much wind or inclement weather, or too much distance can do to lungs, legs, and patience. On the·road, this kind of leader can set the pace and make sure that no one lags far behind and that the group does not scatter hopelessly during rest and meal stops.

After all this you are probably wondering why you can't just go touring alone. For women and young cyclists this is dangerous. You have little defense against thieves or bums. Even for grown men, solo cycling requires a special nature. You might think nothing could be better than getting out on the open road away from everyone, but, after a few hours, you are almost certain to feel lonely. Typically the solo cyclist will cut his trip short. Of course illness and breakdowns can become major disasters for the solo cyclist.

WHAT TO CARRY

If you are touring over several days, you will want to carry at least one change of socks and underwear. The used garments can be washed at the end of the day and hung to dry overnight. In addition to your cycling clothes, you should have at least one change, preferably "dress-up" or at least semiformal clothes. It is surprising how a dress can spark up a girl's spirits at the end of the day. Slacks and a clean shirt will make most boys feel human again too, despite long hours at the pedals. If you go out at night, such clothes will be needed to feel comfortable in most communities. The new drip-dry, wrinkle-proof clothes are by far the best bet for alternate wear on touring. They pack easily and don't look as if you have wrestled a bear in them when you put them on. Knickers and long socks, good for cold-weather cycling, make passable street wear, but even if this style suits you, you will still want a change at the end of the day. I also recommend a spare pair of shoes, comfortable ones for walking. The best would be dressy enough to wear with streets clothes but have hard rubber soles so they could be used for pedaling if your regular shoes give out.

With the informal trends in today's clothing, some will argue with the above suggestions. With clothing, of course, you must suit yourself, but do change at the end of the day. That sweat-soaked jersey worn constantly can give cyclists a bad name as well as a bad smell.

You may want to carry pajamas. Again, the drip-dry type are best. A raincoat can double as a bathrobe, but unless you expect bad weather, a raincoat is superfluous.

Your kit should include toothbrushes, combs, and other toilet gear. For shaving, the battery-powered razors are best on a tour. Girls should carry lotions and cosmetics in plastic bags to guard against leakage. Bar soap is far handier than liquids or powders. You can flake it with a knife for the nightly laundry.

As for cold weather, a sweater is the most useful garment both on the bike and off. Beginning cyclists often get too bundled up at the start of a cold morning. Within a few minutes they are wringing wet and have to stop to stow the extra duds away. For very cold touring, heavy socks, long underwear, sweat pants, a sweater, and a windbreaker might not keep you warm enough. A newspaper across your chest under the windbreaker can cut the chill breeze and hold in body heat. Earmuffs or woolen caps can be mighty comforting. The first extremities to complain in the cold are usually your feet. If thick or extra socks don't solve the problem, you might try the battery-heated socks that sport shops sell to duck hunters.

During a rain, you can see people wearing just about anything on a bicycle from trench coats to oilskin rain suits. Flapping ponchos are the choice of some, because they double as ground covers or bike covers. The cape is better, but it does not protect the feet. Hard-working cyclists soon give up the oilskins, because they restrict evaporation and become as wet with perspiration inside as they are on the outside. If you are hardy and don't mind a soaking, at least not in warm weather, you might just forget about rain gear and count on drying out when the skies clear. This sounds Spartan, but many old hands at touring follow this practice, reasoning or perhaps rationalizing that getting wet is part of the cycling experience. If you adopt this method, the only extra cycling clothes you will want will be a sweater and a windbreaker.

HOW TO PACK

In loading gear on a bicycle, the rule to remember is keep a low center of gravity. This is why saddlebag containers hung from wire racks are so popular with touring cyclists. You can buy them for both front and rear, but the front bags should be about half the size of the rear. If you carry a sleeping bag, one of the light, mummy type, it can be strapped to the top of the rear rack without unbalancing the bike. In addition to saddlebags, you can also buy bags that strap on the rear of the seat and on the handlebars. Handlebar bags are a handy place for warm clothing and snacks that you may want on the road, but keep this bag light.

Your touring bike, with an air pump and tool kit, should weigh little more than thirty pounds. The cargo should not outweigh the bike. In other words, forty pounds of cargo on a thirty-pound bike would be ten pounds too much. It can be and is done, but if you and your companions find that your cargoes outweigh your bikes, you should consider a sag wagon.

The sag wagon is a car, station wagon, or pickup, maybe even a bus, that travels the route with you. It can relieve you of extra gear. It can also pick up tired cyclists (and their bikes) unable to continue pedaling to the evening's destination. On some tours cyclists take turns driving the sag wagon. On others a friend or a parent drives as full-time duty. I advise beginning tourers who attempt challenging trips to travel with a sag wagon. The sag wagon not only can pick you up if you tire, but it can rescue the cyclist with mechanical break-down.

WHAT ABOUT FOOD?

There are few tours that will take you far from a grocery store. There is thus usually no need to carry large supplies of food. If you must carry enough for one or two meals, avoid cans and glass containers. Look into the dehydrated preparations carried in sporting-goods stores for back packers. These foods are expensive, but the saving in weight makes them worth the price. Many tourers at the start of the day prepare a picnic lunch, and most carry energy-building snacks to eat en route. Candy bars give quick energy but no bulk. Dried fruits and firm fresh fruits such as apples are popular. Avoid soft fruits such as peaches or oranges, which may have to be spooned out of your pack. Pretzels or salty crackers are the choice of some cyclists, who need to replace salt lost through perspiration. Others swear by "gorp," an equal mixture of raisins, chocolate bits, and salted peanuts. You may not be in the habit of eating between meals, but on a day of cycling you will most likely find a need for these quick-energy snacks. The salty stuff will make you thirsty, however, so don't forget to fill your water bottle at the start of the day.

WHERE TO STAY

You can stay at hotels or motels, enjoy luxuriant rest, and spend a good deal of money. Sometimes these are the only accommodations available, but for most of us the expense is restrictive. A complaining budget usually heads us for home before complaining muscles influence us.

If you don't need great luxury, want to hold expenses to a minimum, and like the companionship of other travelers, then look into hosteling.

Hosteling began in 1909, when Richard Schirrmann, an elementary-school teacher in Germany, started taking his city-bound pupils on excursions into the country. Travel was no expense, because the children hiked, but reasonable overnight shelter was hard to find until Schirrmann hit upon the idea of converting unused buildings into dormitories. The idea spread. People began offering buildings where hikers could cook, wash clothes, and sleep. Other European countries soon had hostels, and in 1932 representatives of the movement from these countries met in Holland for the First International Hosteling Conference. Each country would recognize hostel membership of other countries; each would stick to high standards of sanitation and safety; each would assure responsible wardens in each shelter. There would be no alcoholic beverages allowed in shelters. Smoking would be confined to common rooms. Members would be expected to supply their own sleeping bags or sleeping sheets. With these international standards established, hosteling spread even faster.

In 1934, Isabel and Monroe Smith, schoolteachers and scout leaders, established the first United States hostel, in Northfield, Massachusetts. Others followed, in Vermont and New Hampshire, the next year. Hostels have been added steadily every year. Today there are more than a million youth-hostel members. There are a total of 4,317 shelters in forty-seven different countries, with 115 of these in the United States and sixty in Canada. An annual pass for juniors, those under eighteen years old, is five dollars; all others, ten dollars. With these passes you may have overnight accommodation for $.40 to $1.25 abroad, and $1.50 to $2.00 in the United States and Canada.

Do not let "youth" mislead you. Travelers of all ages enjoy hosteling. The only requirement is that you travel under your own power: either by hiking, canoeing, or cycling.

CHOICE OF TOURS

In addition to providing shelters, American Youth Hostels organizes tours for its members in nearly every country of the world. It also puts out much specific information on trips. The most valuable guide offered by the AYH to date is Warren Asa's *North American Bicycle Atlas*, which provides maps and directions for nearly one hundred and fifty different tours. Information on hostel membership and publications can be obtained by writing the national headquarters, at 20 West 17th Street, New York, N.Y. 10011.

Several other organizations sponsor tours at home and abroad at reasonable rates. One of them, the International Bicycle Touring Society, came into being practically by accident in 1964 when Dr. Clifford L. Graves, a California surgeon, invited cyclists to join him on a tour of New England. The crowd that turned out, much larger than expected, had such a good time that they organized the society. Organization of a society tour is done by volunteers without pay, but

From a mansion to an old coast-guard station, you can find shelter in almost every kind of building if you take up hosteling. The mansion is the Washington, D.C., International Youth Hostel, just eight blocks from the White House. The coast-guard station is the Star of the Sea Hostel, on Nantucket Island. Courtesy American Youth Hostels, Inc.

accommodations are somewhat more expensive than hostel shelters. Information can be had by writing the International Bicycle Touring Society, 846 Prospect Street, La Jolla, Calif. 92037. The society does not accept membership from anyone under twenty-one.

Most bicycle clubs sponsor tours in their localities. Often these are special day events that attract cyclists from many other clubs and areas. The sponsoring clubs provide maps and information and usually give out jacket patches to those who complete the tours. Collecting tour patches is part of the fun of cycling.

Such club touring has rapidly gained popularity, with the number of tours and entries climbing each year. The tours are far too many to list, but they usually are extremely well organized, with special precautions taken for safety. The Bikeway Tour of the Erie Canal, sponsored by the Onondaga Cycling Club, of Syracuse, New York, and the Syracuse Optimist Club, is typical. The fourth annual staging of this event was held August 5, 1972, and James L. Konski, Onondaga's president, reported 560 entries for the fifty-mile ride from Syracuse to Rome. All but five cyclists completed the run. The youngest to finish was five years old, the oldest sixty-eight. All Onondaga members act as marshals in the event, and any cyclist seen riding unsafely is disqualified. None were, and Konski reported that none lost his way.

"It has been a growing success every year," he said.

The only odd occurrence on the 1972 tour was a sag wagon's pickup of an exhausted woman cyclist who, as it turned out, was not participating in the event.

T. Robert Mayer, president of the Baltimore Bicycling Club, organized the Maryland-Delaware Flatland Tour in 1971. It drew seventy-five cyclists that year, and in 1972 it drew two hundred, and this on a rainy day. "I am certain that the amount of people would have at least doubled if it had been a clear day," Mayer said. The tour is offered with a choice of three loops—of twenty, fifty and seventy miles—and it is just one of four tours sponsored each year by the Baltimore club.

The North Roads Bicycling Club, of Rice Lake, Wisconsin, formed in 1968 with a total "fleet" of six bikes, now sponsors several tours and races, but its members also point proudly to routes in the region open to informal use at any time. North Roads president W. R. Pearson states that the Tuscobia Trail, following an abandoned railroad right of way for seventy-six miles from Rice Lake to Park Falls, Wisconsin, is the "best bet" in the area.

Club tours are often advertised in bicycle magazines and newsletters. The best way to get the schedule of tours, however, is to belong to a club that maintains good exchange of information with other clubs and their activities.

HOW TO TRAIN

Do not start a tour, even a short day tour, if you are not used to pedaling the required distance. Take time to get in shape, and train gradually. Many cyclists work out without any baggage on their bikes only to discover after they have loaded up for the tour that their saddlebags are like anchors. Wise cyclists get in practice carrying extra weight on their bikes.

If bad weather keeps you indoors prior to a tour, you can get special roller platforms, which allow you to pedal your bike in place. Of course if you have use of a stationary exercise bike, you have an excellent way to keep in condition. Try to discover your best cycling cadence when doing these indoor exercises. Lacking a roller platform or an exercise bike, you should at least follow a routine of calisthenics.

Sore knees are a common complaint of beginning tourists, and the soreness is usually due to improper cycling: bending the knees outward instead of keeping them in line with the vertical plane of the body as you pedal. Bending the knee could be due to a seat adjusted too low for your legs, or there might be luggage or gear stowed improperly. Nothing should interfere with the power drive of your legs.

If you can possibly avoid it, do not start a tour with a brand-new bike. In the first place, few bikes are exactly the same, and, no matter how experienced you are, it takes time to grow accustomed to a new machine. In the second place, new bikes have a way of developing problems in the first few hundred miles. New brake and shifting cables stretch; new brake shoes sometimes squeak, and new saddles nearly always feel like bricks. These may sound like minor problems, but they can be annoying, at best. At the worst, you can be sidelined with a bottom so sore that your eyes bulge. Sore bottoms, in fact, vie with sore knees as the leading complaint of beginning cyclists.

If you must use a new saddle, soak the underside with a leather conditioner such as neat's-foot oil, and attack the top side with a rolling pin or a baseball bat to take some of the stiffness out of the seat. This may sound silly, but it works. It can keep you out of the sag wagon.

SPECIAL PROBLEMS

With a loaded bike, you will want to use extra caution in braking. On a long downhill run, brakes will get hot if applied steadily. This can glaze the rims, causing slippage, and the heat can reduce the life of your tires. Experienced cyclists develop a braking rhythm, repeatedly applying and releasing the brakes, always in unison. Coaster brakes should be used with similar rhythm on a hill if you are carrying a load.

Tires wear faster on a loaded bike, and punctures are more likely. Many tourists carry an extra tube as well as a tube patch kit. As a further precaution, you can buy punctureproof tubes, which will save you from trouble even on rough ground. Such tubes should be considered a must if you tour in the American Southwest, where puncture vines and cactus spines can raise havoc with ordinary tubes.

Do not cycle with heavy knapsacks or packs on your back. This throws extra weight on your seat and the handlebars. You will not pedal efficiently with this weight, and you surely will tire early. Many cycling jerseys have pockets for spare gear and equipment. These are handy, but do not overload them. Cameras present a special packing problem on a tour. They do not ride well in saddlebags. Jolting can put them out of adjustment, and bags seem to produce bales of lint and dust just for cameras. They are best carried on your back or in a jersey pocket, but make sure the camera does not swing or bounce against your body as you pedal.

Often city dwellers are encircled by miles of traffic and networks of freeways, which prevent them from cycling to good touring country. One solution is a car with a bike carrier or a pickup truck. If neither of these is available, look into train service. Some railroads run special trains for cyclists, allowing you and your bike to board together. On most trains, you can send your bike in the baggage car while you ride in a passenger car behind. Make sure, however, that you and the bike get off at the same station. There are a few clubs in the nation that have acquired buses to take members and their bikes to touring country. These are ideal, and if there is enough touring interest in your club, you might help promote such a purchase.

Airlines, which have long resisted uncrated bikes as baggage, have finally recognized that touring cyclists are here to stay. For a time, some lines absolutely refused bikes, while others would not take them unless you signed a damage waiver. Now the major lines are competing to attract cyclists. American Airlines, for instance, charges four dollars to eight dollars freight for a bike, depending on the distance, and what's more, offers a heavy plastic shipping cover for an extra two dollars.

8. Camping

Nearly everything said about touring applies to bike camping. In addition, there are some special things you should know and do to make the camping trip a success.

Invariably, the beginning camper tries to carry too much on his bike. Even after you read this chapter, you will undoubtedly be overloaded on your first camping trip. On your second trip, you will leave behind the things that had little or no use on the first trip, and the third time out, your kit will be close to the bare necessities. Actually, this is one of the great satisfactions of camping. In a world of gadgets, luxuries, and canned entertainment, man can still prove his independence and self-reliance by going camping.

Advertisements tell us we cannot survive without certain hair creams or lotions, that our health depends on a certain breakfast food, that we haven't lived until we've tried some sticky concoction of syrup and soda water. Is it any wonder that camping is more popular than ever?

Camping puts the world back in its correct proportions. Man is not such a complicated creature, after all. He does not need wealth and great possessions to appreciate his environment.

Still you are going to pack too much on that first camping trip.

ESSENTIALS

You will need a sleeping bag or a blanket roll. A good sleeping bag, the mummy type, weighing about three pounds, is expensive, but it is worth it if you know you will be a frequent camper. If you are testing camping as a new experience, you would probably be wise to use a blanket or quilt on your first overnight venture. You might want to make a sleeping bag by folding and sewing a blanket, but the bedroll and the homemade bag, while they can keep you comfortable on summer nights, are bulkier and heavier than most bags you can buy.

You will also want some kind of ground cover. The earth cools at night. It will cool you too if you do not have a ground cover to retain your body heat. The cover also will help keep your bag and clothes clean. Some bike campers use ponchos for ground covers. Ponchos serve well, but I prefer something bigger, with enough extra material to cover the bag in case of heavy morning dew or light rain. Very light plastic, eight by ten feet, folds into a small package, and if you hit rain in your travels, you can roll your sleeping bag with the plastic around it for waterproofing.

Your toilet kit should include toothbrush, cake soap, comb, and towel. Tooth paste has a pesky way of escaping from its tube while packed. Carry tooth powder instead. Campers should also carry a roll of toilet paper. Campground toilets are so often bankrupt of this commodity that it is a mistake to depend on them.

You will also want a pocket knife, but don't carry a bulky model that will chafe your leg while cycling. Matches in a waterproof container and a small compass should be recommended as essentials for each camper, but I must confess that I often let someone else carry them. One central container of matches and one compass in a party will serve very well if you do not plan solo hiking.

In addition to the individual necessities, every camping party will need a cooking kit and utensils. The nesting aluminum pots, pans, plates, and cups are convenient in camp. Most kits include six plates and cups. These, however, are bulky to load, and they rattle like Spanish castanets on the road. Individual mess kits, with one community frying pan, one large pot, and a coffee pot, have been most satisfactory for our needs. In addition you will want eating utensils, a spatula, two tablespoons, one sharp knife, two dish towels, and two pot holders. Pliers from your tool kit can be used to lift hot pots, but the pot holders do not add much weight.

Each party should have at least one tote bag for carrying and storing food. The net, stretch-type bags are best, but an old pillow cover will work just as well. This leads to the whole question of camping food. You can carry everything you need for every meal on your bike, provided the trip is not too long and you use the previously mentioned dehydrated preparations. But is this necessary? It is not, unless you are camping in some wilderness far beyond the last country market. Such wilderness areas are extremely rare. Most camp sites, in fact, are seldom more than a half hour of pedaling from a grocery. Here's where the tote bag comes in. You will also want to use the tote bag for storing food at night out of reach of animals. By animals I mean everything from ants to bears. Use some rope or stout cord. Tie one end to your cache of groceries and throw the other end over a limb. Then hoist the groceries. You should get them at least ten feet off the ground.

A resident of California's Sequoia National Park taught me the importance of tote-bag grocery storage. This particular resident was a huge brown bear who visited our camp in the middle of the night. If you have ever cowered in your sleeping bag listening to a bear go crunching and smacking through your supplies, you, too, know the importance of caching food. Even if you leave camp for a few hours during the day, cache your food.

Each camping party should have an ax and a shovel. The U. S. Forest Service requires campers to carry shovels for fire fighting. Light shovels with folding handles like those carried on a soldier's pack are best for bike camping. Your ax should have a case or guard to keep it from slicing through things in your pack.

The camp light is largely a matter of choice. If you plan to read at night, you will want a powerful battery light, a butane type, or a primus type using white gas. Big batteries are heavy, and they wear out. The butane and primus lights use mantles, which do not last in bike packing; you must carry spares. In addition, the gas needed for the primus light will leak from the lamp' or the storage container if you are not extra-careful. At best, this gives everything in your pack a gassy stink. At worst, you could suffer an explosive fire. Personally I prefer cheap candles, available in any grocery, for camp lights. Other lighting comes from removable bike lamps or small flashlights, but these should be used just occasionally, to save batteries.

Each party should have at least one first-aid kit and someone who knows how to use it. Neat gauze bundles, germicides, and smelling salts all stowed in a fancy box cannot substitute for knowledge. Campers should know how to stop bleeding, give artificial respiration, and treat burns, shock, and heat prostration. You can do all these things without fancy medicines or bandages. I find that the simple band-aid for blisters and small cuts is the thing most often sought from our first-aid kit.

LUXURIES

Some of you may argue with the things listed under this heading. They may sound like necessities, and at times, I'll admit, some of them are.

For instance, you may not be able to sleep without an air mattress or a foam-rubber pad. Older campers with sore muscles and worn joints find this particularly true. The younger ones often seem able to bed down on boulders and wake up refreshed. Of course the natural bed of pine needles or leaves will give you a comfortable sleep, but collecting suitable bedding always takes more time and trouble than the woodcraft books lead you to believe. I admit that I carry an air mattress, but I still regard it as a luxury.

Tents also border between luxury and necessity. Whether or not you carry a tent depends almost entirely on the weather patterns in your area. If forecasts are reliable and you can count on fair weather for weeks at a time, leave the tent behind and sleep under the stars. On the other hand, if the weather prophets in your region are constantly embarrassed by nature and surprise storms are the rule, then pack a tent. There are many types and sizes. The family tent with full headroom, unless you pull a bike trailer, is too big for bike camping. The two-man or the one-man pup tent is about right, but if these represent too big an expense, consider a simple tent shelter you can hang on ropes between trees at your camp site. These will keep your sleeping quarters dry, and they do not have that tent stuffiness, a real advantage in my book.

Unless you camp where wood gathering and wood fires are prohibited, stoves are also luxuries. As with lamps, stoves can be had with white gas or butane fuel. A few of the designs are handy and light, but most are bulky rattlers for bike camping. Jellied fuels such as Sterno do not give hot flame, but a can or two will add convenience in boiling tea or soup on a lunch stop. The wood-fire camper avoids all the trouble and expense of stoves, and at the same time, appreciates more of that self-reliance we've been talking about. Most public camps have grates or simple stoves for wood fires. You must, of course, be careful to put your fire out when you leave camp. The only bad mark against wood fires is the mark they leave on cooking pots and pans. Open flame leaves a layer of soot that no amount of scrubbing will remove. You will want to pack your pans in a paper sack or an old bag to keep this soot off your other gear.

WHERE TO CAMP

The most important consideration in selecting a camp is water. Choose the side of a stream or lake or a place where water has been piped in for your camp site. Water has the disadvantage of attracting mosquitoes and gnats. Sometimes these pests are so bad that no amount of repellent or wood smoke gives relief. You may have to choose a new site. Unfortunately water near "civilized" regions is not always fit to drink. If there is any doubt, boil the water before using it. Sporting-goods stores sell purification tablets, which are handy for brief stops en route when you don't want to go to the trouble of a fire.

Other things to look for in picking a site include sun and shade. Some canyon sites are so shaded you'll feel like a troll by the second day. Others, on flat, treeless country, get baked by the sun. The open sites also are subject to wind, and wind can make camp housekeeping an ordeal.

Most established camp sites on public lands are well located, but once in a while you will come upon one that seemingly was chosen by some deskbound bureaucrat. A little experience with a bad camp will make you an expert at site selection.

You should know the regulations covering camping in your area. National Park and Forest Service camps now require a daily fee. Many state-park camps cannot be had in summer months without reservations. In nearly all cases, campers are required to register and carry campfire permits.

As a final word on camping, get some general tips from some of the many camping books available at the bookstore or the library. While few deal with bike camping specifically, the information in the books gives more detail than can be included here. If you like cooking, get a book of camp recipes to add to your fun. The bibliography in the back of this book names some of the best camping books.

9. Competition

Few sports demand as much dedication as bicycle racing. The life of a racer usually includes up to eight hours of training a day, a strict diet, and early bedtime. In Europe, where bicycle racing has long been a professional sport, young men burn themselves out physically and mentally, vying for the big money. All too many use drugs to suppress pain and fatigue, and most of the drugs are addictive.

In America, fortunately, racing today is an amateur sport, and while the contestants take it seriously and work hard at their training, the American racers do not destroy their bodies for the sake of competition. Even so, the beginning cyclist should take a long, hard look at serious racing before he takes it up as his sport. Later in this chapter we will take a look at racing. Meanwhile there are many other ways you can have fun and improve your skill in competition.

THE BIKE RODEO

Recreation departments, service clubs, or merchant groups in cities and towns across the country sponsor bike rodeos. If

none has yet been started in your neighborhood, then maybe
it is time you organized one.

You need a large, smooth surface. Schoolyards or roped-off
parking lots are ideal. A dark, paved surface that will show
chalk or lime markings is perfect. The nature of events possible
in a bike rodeo practically has no limit. You will probably
want to invent some contests of your own. Here are a few
suggestions.

Straight riders—Over a fifty-foot course draw two parallel
lines six inches apart. Contestants must pedal between the
lines without touching them. A wheel on the chalk disqualifies
the rider. No running starts are allowed. The front wheel must
be between the lines when the contestant starts pedaling. For
novices, make the lines a foot apart. This race is more difficult
than it sounds. It should be advertised as a safety test.

The spiral—Draw a spiral with about two feet between the
lines. Contestants must ride to the center of the spiral without
crossing the line.

The slalom—This has many variations. Generally it should be
a zigzag course between parallel lines marked with chalk or
string, with the angle for each turn shallow or sharp, depending on the skill of the contestants. Instead of using chalk or
string, you can mark each turn with a stake, or pylon. Contestants take the course one at a time, racing against the clock.
Touching a line or a marker disqualifies the contestant. One
variation calls for coffee cans at each turn and a collection of
marbles. The rider must drop a marble in each can as he runs
the course. If you don't think this takes concentration, try it.

Sprints—Run sprints from a standing start over tracks five
hundred to one thousand feet long on either an oval or a
straightaway. You can start several contestants at a time, but
the track should be at least thirty feet wide to avoid crowd-
ing. Winners can be determined through elimination heats.

The relay—The usual form of relay racing calls for one bike
for each team. The starter races for a set distance to give the
bike to the second member of the team and so on until the end
of the race. Running more than three teams at once will crowd
most tracks. This is an excellent spectator event. As a variation,
you can have each team member on his own bike with the

relay made by passing a baton, and if you really want to make it difficult, have the baton a lemon held on a teaspoon.

Coasting—After a set distance to get up speed, the contestant must stop pedaling at a fixed mark and see how far he can make his bike coast. Quality and condition of the bike comes into play here, so it will be a much better contest if each entrant uses the same machine.

The slug race—Anyone who can balance his bike for minutes at a time without moving will have a good chance at winning the slug race. The idea is to travel a fixed distance in the longest time. Incidentally, don't expect to break the world's record at this one. Tsugunobu Mitsuishi, of Tokyo, Japan, took that prize in 1965 by balancing his bike without moving for five hours and twenty-five minutes.

Speed braking—You will need a straightaway of about a hundred feet for this. At twenty-five feet from the finish, draw a chalk line. This is the brake point. Contestants must speed into the course and not hit the brakes until reaching the brake line. They are to bring their bikes to a stop without skidding, before hitting the finish line. You may have trouble with some who hold back on their speed in this race. Use a pace bike with each racer. If the contestant does not keep up with the pace bike, disqualify him.

Balance race—You have probably practiced walking with a book or a light board on your head. Try a race with each rider balancing a board on his head. This is too rough for books.

Newspaper toss—Contestants who have a paper route will do best at this. A blanket hung between two trees or posts makes a good target. Each rider has two folded newspapers. He must throw them one at a time at the target as he rides over a fixed route. Best marksman wins.

Other events—You might want to open your rodeo with a *bicycle parade*, giving prizes for the best decorations and the most unusual bikes. You can decorate your bike with colored cardboard disks on the wheels, or you can weave crepe paper between the spokes. Banners and streamers will also brighten a parade, and if you have access to them, try flowers on your bike. A *scavenger chase* on bikes might be a good way to end your rodeo. Take care, however, that the chase does not lead into or across heavily traveled streets.

For a successful rodeo, you want enough variety in events so that novices can take part, and, at the same time, skillful riders are challenged. Six-year-olds cannot be expected to compete against ten-year-olds. Make divisions by age groups. Many rodeos are staged with separate divisions for boys and girls. This is not always necessary, unless the aim is to keep boys from being humiliated. In the growing process, girls usually reach full co-ordination and stamina sooner than boys. Why not leave events open to both sexes and enjoy some surprises?

CROSS-COUNTRY

Cross-country racing attracts cyclists young and old. You must be tough, however, and you will not enjoy this event if you can't stand a little dirt and perhaps a few bruises. Adults call this cyclo-cross. They use special bikes with chain guards and high brackets to keep the drive out of mud and dirt. Sometimes the cyclo-cross course is as much as eight miles long. Younger racers get by with their own bikes, provided they are rugged; and the course does not have to be nearly as long for a good contest.

A rugged cross-country race will include mud and water hazards, hills, barriers such as stacked bales of hay or fences, and thick foliage. In a tough contest, the racer rides, carries, and drags his bike. Of course, in selecting a cross-country course, it helps to find as many natural barriers as possible, such as a shallow stream and thickets of brush. Building a water hazard or a sandbank is hard work and can run into expense. Cross-country is really a mixture of bike riding and running. It will take a lot out of you, but it is even rougher on bikes, so don't use an expensive lightweight or utility bike in this event. Novelty bikes and heavyweights are the machines for cross-country. You can run these races with separate starts and time each contestant, or you can use a mass start and watch the scramble.

HILL CLIMB

Do not select a hill for this sport that is so steep no rider can top it. The grade should be challenging but climbable, and there should be a level stretch at the base so riders can gain speed on the approach. Start contestants individually, and time each. Each rider should have three or four tries for best time.

BICYCLE POLO

The first game of bicycle polo was played in County Wicklow, Ireland, on October 4, 1891. The sport has gained popularity in the British Isles steadily ever since. In the United States the first game was played at Hamilton, Massachusetts, in 1897. Its history in America has been spotty. Interest in the sport all but died when the bicycle craze died at the end of the nineteenth century, but one group of youngsters kept it alive; they were the students at Aiken Preparatory School, at Aiken, South Carolina. In the 1930s other schools and clubs took up the game, and its popularity grew until World War II. Just as the revival began to die, the United States Bicycle Polo Association was created. Again the Aiken students kept the sport alive, during the war years, and when peace came, graduates introduced the sport at the university level. Today interest continues to grow along with the bicycle boom.

The game, of course, is modeled after horse polo, but there are several differences. The rectangular playing field is smaller than a horse-polo field. For bicycle polo, the maximum length should be a hundred ten yards, the width sixty yards. Smaller dimensions will do if you don't have this kind of space. Goals are marked by two posts, twelve feet apart, at each end of the field.

You will want a regulation polo ball (a four-ounce sphere made of bamboo or willow root) and polo mallets with the handles cut down to thirty inches. Games have been played with croquet equipment, but these are slow games compared with those played with polo gear. The object is to get the ball through the opponent's goal.

There are four men on a team, two playing forward, or offense, position and two playing back to defend the goal. Each player may hit the ball no more than three times in succession. No player may block or use any physical contact to force another player away from the ball. This last rule is designed to save damage to both players and bikes.

Play is run in periods or chukkers of seven and a half minutes each. To start play, the referee counts backward from five, and on "zero" rolls the ball on the centerline between the teams. The same countdown is used to resume play after the ball has gone out of bounds. The referee may also call fouls and award free shots. You may not hit the ball with your foot and you may not hit while dismounted. Neither foot may touch the ground.

Best bike for the game is a stripped utility model or a novelty bike. Some players cut the handlebars short on one side to cut down interference with their swings at the ball. Others put shields in the wheels to protect spokes. Further information on bicycle polo can be had by writing the United States Bicycle Polo Association, Box 565 F. D. R. Station, New York, N.Y. 10022.

RACING

Bicycle races fall into two classes: track racing and road racing. Generally competition in either class follows two different forms. Contestants can race for speed over a measured distance, or they can race for distance against a fixed time.

All serious races in the United States are run under the rules of the Amateur Bicycle League of America. To enter these races, you must be licensed by the A.B.L. of America. For information on applying for a license, find who represents the A.B.L. of America in your area. Bike-shop owners or officers of the local club will know.

The league has established four age divisions for racing. Midgets are twelve years old and under. Intermediates are thirteen through fifteen. Juniors are sixteen and seventeen. Seniors are eighteen and over. Seniors are further divided by ability. C Division is for competitors with brief records or few wins. B Division is for those with longer records and good showings. A Division is for those who have won several races. Men and women compete separately.

As already stated, successful racing requires full dedication. If you already know someone who races, ask his advice before you take racing up as your sport. Many touring cyclists, people interested in travel and fun, cannot understand the attitude of the racing cyclist. The touring crowd may try to dissuade you from serious racing.

If possible, have an experienced racer observe your style, and ask him for an honest opinion. Find out about his own attitude toward the sport. He most likely does not drink or smoke, follows a strict diet and training routine, and devotes little time to other interests. After this, if you are still interested, apply for a license and start training for your first race.

I should warn you at this point that I am not a racer. If I were, this chapter would be far more extensive. I will certainly admit that racing is an exciting sport. At this moment it is among America's fastest-growing sports.

Clubs sponsoring races are finding it difficult to accommodate all the entrants. Newspapers and magazines which ignored the sport through most of the sixties now run stories and pictures of bicycle races. As public knowledge has grown, so have crowds. People have discovered a "new" spectator sport. Indeed, one race, the historic Elgin-Chicago run, was canceled recently because it had become overpopular. The sponsors could no longer handle the increased spectators and entries. This is the exception. The usual story is the announcement of yet another new race, not a cancellation. The Eastern Hills Mall Championship, staged by the Buffalo (New York) Cycling Club, drew eighty contestants at its first run, in 1972. Western New York State's now-famous Patchin Race, expanded in 1972 to a hundred-mile course, was one of three preparation races staged for selection of the United States' Olympic road-racing team.

If you decide to take up racing, one of your first decisions will be between track and road racing. Let's discuss these separately.

The 1972 running of the 100-Mile Road Race at Patchin, New York, saw Olympic contenders competing for a spot on the United States' team. This picture, taken on the first lap, shows the cyclists working up a hill. The race began in 1949 as a ten-mile contest to promote the Patchin Fire Company carnival. Courtesy Lawrence Reade

TRACK RACING

Track racing has two important limitations. First of all, you need a special bike. Secondly, the number of tracks in the United States is limited.

Track bikes have short wheel bases and minimum clearance between frame and wheel. There is no room for fenders, and there are no brakes. They are extremely light, some no more than fifteen pounds. Prices begin at about $225 and go up to five hundred dollars and more.

There are eight competitive bicycle tracks in the United States. They are located at Kissena Park, New York City; St. Louis, Missouri; Northbrook, Illinois; Portland, Oregon; Kenosha and Milwaukee, Wisconsin; and San Jose and Encino, California.

If you take up track racing, you might begin with handicap competition, in which each racer starts at a different point according to ability. These are usually quarter- to half-mile contests.

Match racing gets into tactics. In these races, two and sometimes three contestants of equal ability are started together and circle the track for a set number of laps with just the final few laps or the last lap timed. The trick is to start your sprint for the finish with your opponent out of position. The smart match racer likes to stay behind so that the other racer does not see his move until it is too late. By the time the trailing rider has jumped to the lead, however, his opponent usually recovers soon enough to stay close behind and perhaps overtake him at the finish. Sometimes, cagey racers will bluff a sprint early, forcing the other racer to go all out too early. The man who bluffed reserves his strength for a fast finish.

Pursuit racing is yet another form of track competition. Here two equally matched contestants start at opposite sides of the oval and each tries to overtake the other. Since an overtake is rare, the winner is usually determined by elapsed time. Team pursuit racing with four men to a team calls for precise cycling. Members of the team change the lead with each lap in order to spread the work of breaking the wind. Watching the lead bike in a well-practiced team swing wide on a turn to glide back to position within inches of the trailing bike is a study in rhythm and beauty. There are usually four men on a team, but in Australian pursuit racing there can be as many as eight. Here the members are spaced out around their side of the track at the start. If a racer is overtaken by a member of the other team, he must drop out. Italian pursuit racing, with up to five in each team and several teams on the track at once, calls for the trailing team member to drop out with each lap.

There is an individual race that calls for the trailing cyclist to drop out each lap. It is appropriately called "Devil take the Hindmost." Point-to-point racing calls for sprints during several stages of the race, with points given the winner of each sprint. Then there is the six-day "Madison" with two-man teams, which we have already described. These are just a few of the track races. There are other variations, and your first visit to a track may be confusing. Go with someone who can explain what's going on. As soon as you understand the race and get to know the competitors, track racing becomes exciting.

ROAD RACING

Road races in the United States today are many and varied. Best of all, you should not have to travel far to see one. Sometimes the sponsoring organization manages to have the route blocked off for other traffic during the race, but this is not often possible for the long races.

The time-trial style of racing calls for separate starts for each contestant, with each clocked across the finish separately. Massed-start racing is more exciting to watch. Competitors must use tactics to work out of the pack. There is always danger of collisions and spills.

Racing distances range from sprints over fractions of a mile up to the several-hundred-mile, multiday races. Europe's famous Tour de France, a 2,600-mile course through the rugged Pyrenees, is run over a twenty-two-day period. In America, the Aspen Alpine Cup race, though not as long as the Tour de France, leads competitors over the 12,095-foot Independence Pass, in the Rockies. These are massed-start races, and the competitors are not as interested in the clock as they are in beating the other fellow.

In time trials, either over a measured distance or against a fixed time, the racers are thinking always about beating the record. These are fast races. When a cyclist covers a twenty-five-mile course in close to 50 minutes, he is zipping along at an average of 30 miles an hour. In the twenty-four-hour race in which Dean Patterson of Wisconsin's North Roads Bicycle Club set the national record of 337 miles, in the fall of 1972, he had to average 14 miles an hour. If you don't think that's a fast pace to maintain hour after hour, try it sometime.

If you hope to hit this pace, and every serious racer does, start training now. You cannot begin soon enough. With few exceptions, most racers are "over the hill" by the time they reach thirty years. Your peak years will be in the early twenties, and most of today's top racers have years of experience behind them by the time they reach their peak. So if racing a bike is your sport, take a deep breath and begin.

For the winterbound cyclist, an exercise bike can keep legs and lungs in top form. Many racers use these machines as part of their daily training, and physical therapists often recommend them for convalescents. Courtesy Schwinn Bicycle Company

10. Care and Repair

Perhaps you consider yourself a poor mechanic. Perhaps the simplest nut-and-bolt combination mystifies you, and talk about socket wrenches and ball bearings leaves you shaking your head. Don't be so sure of your limitations. If your bike ever breaks down on the road, you might be surprised how quickly you will learn bike mechanics.

Of course there are some people who would rather take their bikes apart than ride them. This chapter will be far too basic for such readers. Here we will cover routine maintenance and enough emergency repairs to get you home most of the time.

The most common bike trouble is a flat tire. It is due to poor care, damage on the road, or a combination of both. Let's take a long look at the bicycle tire.

PREVENTION AND CURE OF FLATS

Too much air in a tire can burst it. Too little air can cause a pinched tube or a cracked casing. When you put your weight on a bike with low tires, you also endanger the rims. Hitting a rock or a chuckhole might bend rims if tires are not properly inflated. What is proper inflation?

Many tires today carry the recommended pressure in pounds per square inch imprinted on their sides. If your tires have no such imprinting, you cannot go far wrong with the following guide:

tire size	width	pressure
12″	all widths	35
16″	all widths	40
18″	all widths	45
20 to 26″	1⅜″	55
20 to 26″	1¾″	40
20 to 26″	2⅛″	35
27″	1¼″	70
27″	(sewn on)	85–100 rear
		75–90 front

With experience some cyclists can tell when a tire has enough pressure by squeezing it between thumb and forefinger, but, until you gain such experience, you will need an air gauge. There are small gauges that can be carried in your tool kit, and there are gauges that fit on a hand pump. Such pumps are ideal for inflating bike tires, but they are too bulky to carry with you.

Use extreme caution with air pumps at service stations. Designed for auto tires, these pumps deliver great volumes of air and can burst a bike tire. If you must use such pumps, cover your tire valve with the nozzle no more than an instant at a time as you trigger the air. Watch the pressure gauge constantly. Keep this up until you reach the recommended inflation.

Since air expands when heated, it is a good idea to lower tire pressure about five pounds in hot weather. You should also reduce pressure about five pounds if you must ride over sharp gravel or rough ground.

The life of rubber tires is shortened by changes in temperature and moisture. Tires can wear out while your bike is stored in the garage. One way to prolong their life is to turn the bike over or hang it up to keep all weight off the tires. Don't let the air out prior to storage. Instead, check the pressure periodically and keep it at normal level. That way the tires will hold their shape.

When cycling, you can save yourself much trouble by paying attention to the road surface. Glass, bits of metal, sharp rocks, ruts, and ridges are all puncture makers. All these hazards can be avoided if you see them soon enough. Veteran cyclists often rub a gloved palm on their turning tires as they ride, to clean off grit and other foreign matter that may have become lodged in the treads. If you do not have gloves, at least look at your treads occasionally to make sure they are clean.

Of course, no matter how careful you are, if you cycle long enough, you will eventually get a flat. Here are the steps for repair:

1. Determine if the leak is in the tube or the valve. To do this, reinflate the tire and glaze the mouth of the valve with a film of water or saliva. If a bubble rises, you have a valve leak. Using the pronged top of your valve cap (you should equip your bike with this style of cap), remove the valve core and inspect the rubber at its base. If the rubber is cracked or dried, you need a new core. If not, replace the core and tighten firmly. Retest with air. It could be that the core was loose or improperly seated due to dirt. If no bubble rises, your troubles are over.

2. If the leak is not in your valve, you must remove the tube and patch it. This job can be done without removing the wheel from the bike, but don't try this stunt with your first flat. To remove the front wheel, simply loosen the axle nuts or quick-release skewers on either side of the hub, and lift the wheel from the jaws of the fork. Back wheels are more difficult. Loosen the axle nuts or skewers, slide the wheel forward in the drop-out slots, creating enough slack to remove the chain from the wheel sprocket, and then slide the wheel back and out. With a coaster brake, you must free the brake arm. With dérailleurs, the chain should be on the smallest, outer sprocket before you attempt wheel removal. With three- and five-speed hubs, you must unlink the shift cable: First put the control in high gear for maximum slack, then loosen the lock nut a half turn and back off the cable-adjustment barrel all the way (counterclockwise). Now you can loosen your axle nuts and remove the wheel with the forward-and-back maneuver.

3. During wheel removal, the core should have been out of the valve to allow free escape of air. Squeeze out as much remaining air as possible, then begin prying the wheel from the rim with your tire irons. There is a trick to this, and the job is usually difficult with stiff, new tires. Stand the wheel up with the valve down, at the six o'clock position. Start prying at the top. As you open a gap between rim and tire with one iron, use the other to gain a new purchase three to four inches away. Work around the rim, alternately prying and advancing. When you have removed one side of the tire all the way, reach inside and pull the tube free until just a small section on either side of the valve remains in the tire. With a firm grip over the tire at this point, you can lift the valve from the hole in the rim and remove tire and tube entirely from the wheel.

4. The next step is to find the leak. Replace the valve core and reinflate the tube. If you have a major leak, you will hear a hissing at once and will be able to locate the leak easily. Unfortunately most punctures are more subtle. The best way to spot these leaks is to immerse the tube in water and look for bubbles, but on the road, water is usually not available. Rotate the tube close to your ear. You may hear the leak. If this does not work, check the inside of the tire both by sight and feel for any defect or foreign material that could have caused the leak. If you find something, match the spot against the tube to find the general location of the trouble. Close inspection of the tube may show you suspicious spots. You can test these with a glaze of saliva. If you still cannot find your leak, hunt for water. About 90 per cent of the time, leak hunting is not as difficult as I make it sound, but that 10 per cent can be frustrating. You simply have to persist.

5. Once you have found the trouble spot, you must patch it. If you have wet the tube, dry the area around the leak carefully. Then, using the sandpaper or grater from your patch kit, rough the rubber around the leak. The area you rough should be larger than the patch you intend to use. Next spread rubber cement over the area and allow it to dry to a tacky state. Most patches today come with adhesive guarded by paper that you peel free just before applying the patch. If your patch is not this type, apply rubber cement to it as well.

Roughing the surface of an inner tube around the area of the patch should be done with a light touch, particularly with a metal grater such as the one pictured here. The same job can be done with sandpaper. The idea is to give the rubber cement a base it can grip. Apply the patch when the cement turns tacky. Courtesy Boy Scouts of America

When the cement has become tacky, press the patch firmly over the leak and hold it in place with a tight grip. While waiting for the patch to dry completely, it is a good time to inspect your tire. If there is a nail or a piece of glass imbedded in the tire, it will give you trouble again unless you remove it. You might find a crease or a slice inside the tire that has pinched or worn the tube. This means you will need a new tire, but for emergency repair, you can place a patch over this area in the same way you patched your tube. Now, when all cement has dried, it is a good time, particularly if you have water, to test the tube again. If there was more than one leak or if your patch did not hold, it is best to find out about it before you put everything together again.

6. Generally, assembly is a reversal of the dismantling process. Remounting the tire and tube is not quite this simple, however. Put just enough air in the tube to keep it from creasing. Insert the tube in the tire. Now, holding the rim with the valve hole at top, insert the valve stem and work one edge of the tire onto the rim. This can be done with the fingers. Next, turn the wheel around and work as much of the other side onto the rim as you can with your fingers. Unless the tire is old and pliant, a crescent will resist your efforts. Use one tire iron to hold one end of this crescent on the rim. Then, prying with the other iron, work from the other end of the crescent, reducing it a few inches at a time until the tire is seated entirely on the rim. Inflate the tube to proper pressure, making sure the stem remains centered in the hole through the rim. Then reinstall the wheel.

Avoid using screwdrivers in lieu of tire irons. It can be done, but the chances are you will cut the tube with the sharp edge of the screwdriver. Spoon handles are safer if you are caught without tire irons.

If you are one of those rare beginners who owns a bike with sewn-on tires, you will probably want to carry an extra tire with you to save yourself a patching chore on the road. These tires take very little space and can be folded and tied beneath a saddle until needed. Patching, which requires removal and replacement of stitches, especially thin patches, and much patience, is best done at home. I recommend you carry a spare when touring. Incidentally, sewn-on tires have stems made for European connections. You will want to carry an adapter in order to use American air pumps.

CHAIN TROUBLE

While nowhere near as common as tire trouble, chain trouble will bring you to a halt on the road. Most chain trouble can be avoided through routine inspection and care. Before you start a trip, look at the chain for worn links and dirt. Dirt is the chief enemy of the chain, and many bike riders encourage dirt by overoiling. The oil gathers dust and grime,

Because it does not attract dirt as much as oil does, graphite lubricant works well on bicycle chains. Use oil on other moving parts. Graphite should never be used in hubs. Courtesy Boy Scouts of America

and this fills the links, causing rapid wear. Some experts recommend rubbing an oily rag over the chain rather than applying oil directly. Others say graphite lubricant rather than oil should be used. Whatever you use, you will want to start with a clean chain. Proper cleaning requires removal of the chain, and you cannot get the chain free of the stays without taking it apart.

There are two chain sizes, those one eighth of an inch wide, found on coaster-brake and hub-geared bikes, and those three thirty-second of an inch wide, found on dérailleurs. The wider chain has a master link. Some master links have a snap-off face. Others come with a split face. The narrower, dérailleur chain has no master link. You will need a chain rivet tool to dismantle one of the links. Do not punch the rivet all the way out of both faces. Leaving it in one face will make reassembly

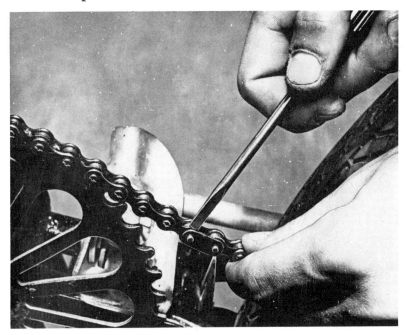

This master link has a snap face, which can be removed with a screwdriver. Pry gently to avoid bending the rivets. Some master links have split faces, which can be pried apart or pulled open with pliers. Courtesy Boy Scouts of America

easier. You reassemble the link with the same tool.

Once the chain has been removed, soak it in a pan of kerosene, taking care not to lose parts of the master link. Work the chain with your hands to free dirt. Stiff links sometimes indicate wear, but you will want to inspect the chain link by link as you work it. Worn links should be replaced, but if there are more than two or three worn ones, you will save yourself present and future trouble by buying a new chain. After cleaning, wipe the chain dry and apply oil or graphite sparingly. Some prefer to lubricate after the chain has been reinstalled.

Many cyclists carry spare links and chain rivet tools with them as part of their kit. This is certainly recommended, particularly on long trips, but make sure you know how to use the tool first. A little practice at home will give you confidence and efficiency when chain trouble strikes on the road.

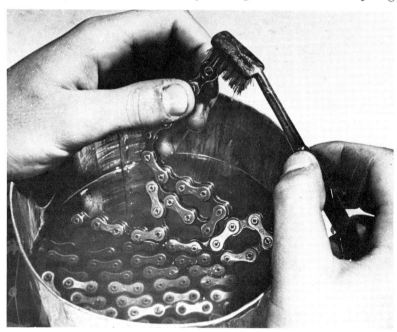

An old toothbrush is ideal when using kerosene to clean your chain. After all the dirt and grit is removed and after you have checked each link for free movement, then lubricate the chain with light oil or graphite. Courtesy Boy Scouts of America

BRAKES

Brake failure carries obvious danger. Never take your bike anyplace without first checking the brakes. Get in the habit of testing brakes before starting down a long hill. Again, proper maintenance can save you grief.

Coaster-brake hubs need a teaspoon of oil three to four times a year. In addition, check to make sure that the bolt clamping the brake arm to the chain stay has not loosened. If you have removed the wheel at any time, you have had to free this brake arm. Make sure it is tightly secured when you replace the wheel. Well-oiled brakes with arms secured should give little trouble, but if you begin to lose braking power, take your bike to the shop. Unless you are an experienced mechanic with special tools, you will be making a mistake opening up a coaster brake. The chances are that some of the complex interior parts are worn and will have to be replaced anyway. Let the shop mechanic handle it.

The expander, or drum, brake found on some tandems and many novelty bikes is activated by a cable attached to a brake arm on the outer face of the drum. Since all cables stretch, your chief concern with these brakes will be in taking up cable slack. Normally you can do this by freeing the lock nut and turning the adjustment barrel counterclockwise. When the cable is nearly taut, reset the lock nut. If this does not do the job, then turn the barrel clockwise all the way and take up cable slack at the anchor bolt on the brake arm.

As we have seen, there are two types of caliper brakes, center-pull and side-pull. Both are subject to cable stretch disease. With center-pulls, the adjustment nut is on a bracket attached to the frame above the brake. Additional slack can be taken up at the anchor bolt located at the yoke above the brake. With side-pulls, the adjustment nut is at the top of the upper brake arm, and the anchor nut is at the end of the bottom brake arm. Often, when adjusting side-pulls, it is necessary to work with both nuts.

With any cable adjustment, no matter how slight, check the brakes afterward. When the brakes are open, the wheel should spin freely without rubbing. The shoes, in fact, should be from an eighth to a quarter of an inch from the rim faces. The shoes should grip the rim evenly when you apply the brakes, and you should not have to depress the control lever more than an inch and a half for the shoes to grip.

Worn shoes on caliper brakes are replaced by undoing the holding nut and removing the shoe and metal holder. While it is a little more expensive to buy new shoes with holders, it is simpler than fitting bare shoes into old holders. A scratch or a bump on the rim face can cause rapid brake wear, as well as brake grab. The problem might be curable with emery cloth on a slight scratch, but if the damage is serious, chances are you will have to replace the rim. Brake grab can cause a harmful spill. A squealing brake is usually caused by grit or a small rock imbedded in the shoe. Clean these things out with a penknife or an ice pick. New shoes will sometimes squeal even if they are clean. It takes some breaking in for them to stop complaining. You can buy polish for your bike, but do not use this stuff on rims. The polish gums the brake shoes. What good is a shining bike if you can't stop it?

Cyclists who have begun on a bike with coaster brakes often find the adjustment to hand brakes difficult. Some using hand brakes for the first time question their efficiency. While it is true that use of hand brakes takes practice and that you cannot lock your rear wheel and throw your bike into a skid with hand brakes, it is unfair to challenge their efficiency. Properly adjusted hand brakes, which put equal pressure on both wheels, give both a wider range and more delicate control than coaster brakes. Hand brakes are the right instrument for a light bike. Imagine *skidding* a light, ten-speed bike to a stop! It is an unsafe way to stop any bike, but with the narrow tires of the light bike, it would be damaging as well.

GEARS, GEARS, GEARS

While it is true that they do not take abuse kindly, gears have earned a reputation for trouble that they don't deserve. Gear problems can often be traced to faulty maintenance or careless handling. If your bike has gears, take a little extra trouble to learn their needs.

There are many makes and models both in the hub and the dérailleur systems. Manufacturers issue maintenance manuals for your particular model. Study the manual carefully, and follow the recommendations. While the comments in this chapter will describe general gear problems and cures, limited space makes it impossible to describe each gear model on the market today. For this detail you want the manual.

Two-speed-hub gears shifted by back pedal pressure need about a teaspoon of light oil once a month. Follow this rule and keep out of deep mud and dust storms, and you should have very little trouble with this hub. Parts will wear after long use. Symptoms of wear include grinding noises and shifting without back-pedaling. If this happens, do not try to dismantle the hub. Unless you are a journeyman mechanic, the intestines of this hub will baffle you. Take the bike to the shop. These hubs, remember, are combined with a coaster brake, and it is a good idea to get them to the shop about once a year anyway, so the mechanic can dismantle, clean, and regrease the brake mechanism.

Problems with three- and five-speed hubs are usually due to lack of oil or to cable stretch. The light oil used in these hubs can evaporate even while the bike sits in the shop showroom. If your bike has been sitting unused for a long period, be sure to oil the hub before jumping on the seat. The routine calls for a teaspoon a month. The innards stick in a dry hub, and the gears will not engage. If oiling does not cure this problem, flush the hub out with kerosene and then reoil. If the gears still stick, take the bike to the shop. These hubs, too, have complex interiors far too awesome for the innocent.

The first indication of cable stretch on a multispeed hub can sometimes be a painful surprise. You can be pedaling along in the middle gear when suddenly your feet spin with no resistance and you either bang your chin on the steering stem or your crotch on the top tube. It is not always quite so bad, but there will be no doubt that something has gone wrong. Dismount, and examine your hub. Most multispeed hubs have arrows or indicator windows on extensions of the axle. Usually these are on the right side of the bike, where the cable control enters the hub, but some models have them on the left.

Make sure the lever or dial on the handlebar is set at the middle gear. If the cable is correctly adjusted, the arrow should be on its mark, or if you have a window model, the end of the indicator rod within the window should be even with the end of the axle. Chances are, these things are not in line. To bring them into adjustment, you must loosen or, more usually, tighten the cable. There are two methods.

First, work with the knurled nut or adjustment barrel just ahead of the hub linkage. Undo the lock nut and then turn the knurled nut or barrel to bring the arrow or indicator rod to its correct position. If the first method does not do the job, then you must move the cable stop on the frame of the bike. This is a clamp on the top tube on boys' models and on the down tube on girls' models. Loosen the clamp and slide it forward or back as necessary.

If the first and second methods both fail, then your cable is either badly frayed or broken, and you need a new one. Remove the cable and take it to the shop, or simply take the bike itself to the shop. Just make sure you get a new cable of the proper length.

On first glance dérailleur systems look complex and intimidating, but as we have already seen, the principle is simple and you can do much more tinkering with dérailleurs than you can with hub gears. Here are common problems and their cures.

The chain may jump off the low, or largest, wheel sprocket and lodge between the sprocket and the metal or plastic spoke protector. The cure calls for adjustment of the low-gear stop screw on the rear dérailleur assembly. Location varies with different models, but the screw is normally near the bottom of the assembly. Refer to your manual if you can't locate it.

The chain may jump from the high, or smallest, wheel sprocket and lodge between the sprocket and the chain stay. The cure calls for adjustment of the high-gear stop screw, usually located at the top of the rear dérailleur assembly. After either type of chain jump, inspect both chain and sprockets for damage. At high speed, a wedged chain can bend sprockets and send you to the shop. Chain jumps can also be dangerous to you if the rear wheel locks. This is good reason for checking gear systems carefully before you start a trip. If your parked bike falls or is knocked over, you can usually expect to do some work on adjustment screws.

As you pedal along, the chain may grind or clatter. The cure for this is to adjust your control levers. It could be that you have positioned the carrier at a middle position between two gears. If this is the case, a slight change up or down will stop the noise.

The chain may slip from a low to a higher gear just as you are beginning an assault on a steep hill. The usual cure for this, after you have gotten over your frustration, is to tighten the wing nut that grips the lever. This, of course, should not be so tight you can't shift, but tight enough to hold the lever where you want it.

You may not be able to shift into low gear. The cure here, if you have already tried solving the problem with the low-gear adjustment screw, is to treat for cable stretch disease: Put the dérailleur in high gear; this is most easily done by turning the bike over onto seat and handlebars. You can turn the pedals with one hand and work the gear lever with the other, a good setup, incidentally, for any gear check or adjustment with a dérailleur. When you have the chain on the smallest, that is, highest, gear, loosen the cable clamp nut on the dérailleur, pull out the slack, and retighten the cable.

The chain may refuse to stay on the sprockets. If all other adjustments seem to be in order, take a close look at the teeth of the sprockets. Worn teeth will throw a chain. The cure here is new sprockets.

Your freewheel mechanism may stick; the wheel will not turn unless the chain and chain wheel turn. This could be caused by dirt jamming the freewheel pawls. Flush the hub with kerosene, and reoil. If this cure does not work, take the bike to the shop. You probably need new parts.

WHEELS

After rough treatment or a long rest, the wheels of a bike can go out of alignment; some spokes will have greater tension than others. This often shows up when you are testing brake shoes. The spinning wheel may brush a shoe for part of the turn. This can indicate serious trouble, but it might simply be that a spoke wrench can fix the problem in a few minutes. Hold a light stick or a pencil against the spokes of the turning wheel. If one or two spokes ping off key, locate them and tighten them with your wrench. Test the wheel again. If it still is out of line, note the spot where it rubs or comes closest to rubbing the brake shoe. Tighten a spoke or two spokes on the opposite side of this spot. Test again. If you still have not solved the problem, I recommend a trip to the shop. You can do a complete wheel-alignment job at home, starting from scratch, with a rim, hub, and stack of spokes, but the shop has a special alignment jig and the experts to do the job.

Do not confuse wheel wobble with alignment problems. If the wheel wobbles from side to side in your grip, it probably means worn bearings in the hub. Check to make sure washers and nuts are tightly seated on the axle. If they are, take the bike to the shop; have a mechanic inspect the hub.

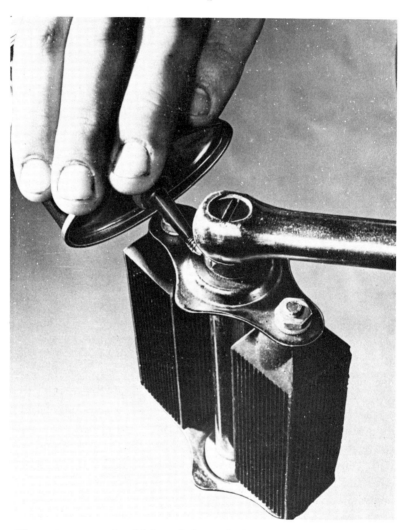

All moving parts should be oiled regularly. Pedals collect dirt faster than any other part of the bike. You can use a brush and kerosene to wash dirt from the spindle, but keep oil and kerosene off the rubber blocks. Courtesy Boy Scouts of America

OVERHAUL

We have already covered most of the light oiling routine. Other moving parts, such as brake pivots on calipers, pedals, dérailleur mechanisms, and handlebar control levers should get drops of oil regularly. Even cables, where they enter guides or tubes, should get a drop of oil. In addition to this, your bike will need major lubrication once a year. Hubs, steering-head bearing assemblies, and chain-wheel axles should be taken apart and greased. Special tools are needed to take freewheel hubs apart, and special tools are often needed on some makes of steering-head assemblies and chain-wheel axles. If you have a knowledgeable friend, one with the proper tools, you can do these jobs at home. If not, I strongly recommend once again that you have them done at a bike shop.

You have perhaps heard veteran cyclists say, "If you can ride it, you can fix it." This may be true for a few, but as a general rule it is misleading, even dangerous. You paid good money for your bike. Professional maintenance and repair will protect that investment.

As a final word, don't get the idea from this chapter that a bicycle is a series of calamities. I have simply tried to cover what can happen, what you can do, and what the mechanic should do to fix it. Actually you will find that your bike will carry you over countless trouble-free miles, that it will give you remarkably few worries, and that you will come to trust it as you would a loyal friend.

Happy traveling!

Bibliography

Asa, Warren, NORTH AMERICAN BICYCLE ATLAS, American Youth Hostels, Inc., New York, 1972.

Bowden, Kenneth, and Matthews, John, CYCLE RACING, Temple Press Books, London, 1965.

Cardwell, Paul, Jr., AMERICA'S CAMPING BOOK, Charles Scribner's Sons, New York, 1969.

Cuthbertson, Tom, ANYBODY'S BIKE BOOK, Ten Speed Press, Berkeley, Calif., 1971.

———, BIKE TRIPPING, Ten Speed Press, Berkeley, Calif., 1972.

Frankel, Godfrey and Lillian, 101 THINGS TO DO WITH A BIKE, Sterling Publishing Co., New York, 1961.

Henkel, Stephen C., BIKES, Bantam Books, Toronto, New York, London, 1972.

Houston, Jack, WANDERING WHEELS, Baker Book House, Grand Rapids, Mich., 1970.

Leete, Harley, ed., THE BEST OF BICYCLING! Trident Press, New York, 1969.

Macfarlan, Allan A., BOY'S BOOK OF BIKING, Washington Square Press, New York, 1970.

Messenger, Charles, CONQUER THE WORLD, Pelham Books, London, 1968.

Murphy, Dervla, FULL TILT, E. P. Dutton & Co., New York, 1965.

Nelson, Janet, BIKING FOR FUN AND FITNESS, Award Books, New York, 1970.

Palmer, Arthur Judson, RIDING HIGH, E. P. Dutton & Co., New York, 1956.

Riviere, Bill, THE COMPLETE GUIDE TO FAMILY CAMPING, Doubleday & Company, Garden City, N.Y., 1966.

Sloane, Eugene A., THE COMPLETE BOOK OF BICYCLING, Trident Press, New York, 1970.

Teeman, Lawrence, ed., BUYER'S GUIDE 1972–1973 BICYCLES AND TEST REPORTS, Doubleday & Company, Garden City, N.Y., 1972.

Wells, George S., THE FUN OF FAMILY CAMPING; A PRACTICAL GUIDE, Bobbs-Merrill Company, Indianapolis and New York, 1962.

Woodforde, John, THE STORY OF THE BICYCLE, Universe Books, New York, 1971.

Index

Though born in Los Angeles, RICHARD B. LYTTLE is really a product of rural California. He graduated from high school in Ojai, served in the Navy in the 1940s, and attended the University of California at Berkeley, where he majored in English and professed boxing as his sport. He graduated with a B.A. degree and several bruises.

Mr. Lyttle has worked as a cowboy, farmer, newspaper reporter, editor, bartender, teacher, and school-bus driver. He began selling stories and articles for children in the 1950s. He sold more than one hundred and fifty articles before turning to books. This is his third book.

The author has retained an interest in sports, particularly sailing, tennis, track and field, and bicycling. He is an enthusiastic camper and trout fisherman.

Mr. Lyttle, his wife Jean, and their two children live in Inverness, a small town north of San Francisco and next door to the Point Reyes National Seashore, where many bike trails invite weekend pedaling.

.3240

629.22 Lyttle, Richard B.
LYT
   The complete
   beginner's guide
   to bicycling

3 2 4 0

DATE			
JAN 21			
APR 25			
MAY 17 '85			
AP 2 90			
NOV 30 2009			
DEC 07 2009